FUNERAL RITES & READINGS

EDITED BY BRIAN MAGEE CM

VERITAS

Published 1995 by
Veritas Publications
7-8 Lower Abbey Street
Dublin 1

ISBN 1 85390 258 6

British Library Cataloguing
in Publication Data.
A catalogue record for
this book is available
from the British Library.

Acknowledgements

Scripture extracts taken from the *Jerusalem Bible,* published and copyright 1966, 1967 and 1968 by Darton Longman & Todd Ltd and Doubleday & Co. Inc., used by permission of the publishers; extracts from *The Psalms: A New Translation,* published by HarperCollins Ltd, reproduced by permission of A. P. Watt Ltd on behalf of the Grail, England; *Ár bPaidreacha Dúchais,* by Diarmuid Ó Laoghaire, cóipcheart © Foilseachán Ábhar Spioradálta, Baile Átha Cliath, 1975; extracts from *Carmina Gadelica,* A Carmichael, are copyright © Scottish Academic Press, Edinburgh, 1972; *Orthaí Cosanta sa Chráifeacht Cheilteach,* Seán Ó Duinn, cóipcheart © 1990 An Sagart, Maigh Nuad; extract from *Prayers Before and After Bereavement* reproduced by permission of McCrimmon Publishing Company Ltd; extract by Gabe Huck reprinted from *A Sourcebook About Christian Death,* copyright © 1990 Archdiocese of Chicago. All rights reserved. Liturgy Training Publications, 1800 North Hermitage Ave, Chicago, IL 60622-1101. 1-800-833-188. Used with permission; extracts from the *Order of Christian Funerals,* copyright © 1985 Committee on English in the Liturgy (ICEL); excerpts from *Pastoral Care of the Sick: Rites of Anointing and Viaticum,* © 1982 ICEL. All rights reserved.

Design: Bill Bolger
Printed in the Republic of Ireland by Criterion Press Ltd, Dublin

Contents

The Funeral Vigil and Related Rites and Prayers

INTRODUCTION

The *Order of Christian Funerals* sees the Catholic funeral liturgy as taking the form of a journey. There is a succession of individual liturgical celebrations within the funeral as a whole, and they take place in different locations. There is a movement to and from home, funeral home, church and cemetery. Sometimes this movement is informal, sometimes in liturgical procession. Some of these liturgies are celebrated by the entire community, some by the bereaved family and friends. They are all seen as being adaptable to time and circumstances. This book contains those prayers and services which are not usually celebrated in the parish church, or expect the presence of a priest. If the priest or deacon is unable to be present because of other serious pastoral obligations, other members of the community should be prepared to assist with these prayers and should have the texts readily available to them. (PCS 213) This book makes these texts and others available to all in this ministry of consolation.

The *Order of Christian Funerals* does not stand alone but is part of the whole sacramental rite of the Church. The Church, as seen in the Rites of Initiation, is a community of faith, of support, of concern, a community constantly inviting others to journey with them.

In the *Pastoral Care of the Sick* that concern is directed towards those who are sick and dying. But that concern is a common concern. It says: *If one member suffers in the Body of Christ, all the members suffer. It is thus especially fitting that all baptized Christians share in this ministry of mutual charity within the Body of Christ by doing all they can to help the sick return to health, by showing love for the sick, and by celebrating the sacraments with them. Like the other sacraments, these too have a community aspect, which should be brought out as much as possible when they are celebrated.* (PCS 33)

A CALL TO EACH MEMBER

In the General Introduction to the new *Order of Christian Funerals* we find that very same quotation from the *Pastoral Care of the Sick*. It continues: '*So too when a member of Christ's Body dies, the faithful are called to a ministry of consolation to those who have suffered the loss of one whom they love. Christian consolation is rooted in that hope that comes from faith in the saving death and resurrection of the Lord Jesus Christ. Christian hope faces the reality of death and the anguish of grief but trusts confidently that the power of sin and death has been vanquished by the Risen Lord. The Church calls each member of Christ's Body – priest, deacon, layperson – to participate in the ministry of consolation, to care for the dying, to pray for the dead, to comfort those who mourn.*' (8)

RESPONSIBILITY OF ALL

'The responsibility for the ministry of consolation rests with the believing community, which heeds the words and example of the Lord Jesus: Blessed are those who mourn; they shall be consoled'. To make this ministry and responsibility clear, it is stated that 'information on how the parish community assists families in preparing for funerals should also be provided.' (9)

The community ministry of consolation is spelt out: 'The faith of the Christian community in the resurrection of the dead brings support and strength to those who suffer the loss of those whom they love.'(9)

ACTS OF KINDNESS

With words of faith are also included 'acts of kindness, for example, assisting them with some of the routine tasks of daily living. Such assistance may allow members of the family to devote time to planning the funeral rites with the priest and other ministers and may also give the family time for prayer and mutual comfort.' (10) 'The community's principal involvement in the ministry of consolation is expressed in its active participation in the celebration of the funeral rites...'(11)

MINISTRY OF THE PRIEST

Ministry to the bereaved is not just the task of the priest, though his ministry is vital: 'by giving instruction, pastors and associate pastors should lead the community to a deeper appreciation of its role in the ministry of consolation and to a fuller understanding of the significance of the death of a fellow-Christian.' (9) The priest should provide information to families and invite everyone to participate in the funeral Mass, being mindful of non-Catholics and of Catholics 'who are not involved in the life of the Church'.

Commendation of the Dying

INTRODUCTION

Into your hands, Lord, I commend my spirit.

In viaticum the dying person is united with Christ in his passage out of this world to the Father. Through the prayers for the commendation of the dying the Church helps to sustain this union until it is brought to fulfilment after death.

Christians have the responsibility of expressing their union in Christ by joining the dying person in prayer for God's mercy and for confidence in Christ. In particular, the presence of a priest or deacon shows more clearly that the Christian dies in the communion of the Church. He should assist the dying person and those present in the recitation of the prayers of commendation and, following death, he should lead those present in the prayer after death. The minister may choose texts from among the prayers, litanies, aspirations, psalms, and readings provided in this chapter, or others may be added. In the selection of these texts the minister should keep in mind the condition and piety of both the dying person and the members of the family who are present. The prayers are best said in a slow, quiet voice, alternating with periods of silence. If possible, the minister says one or more of the brief prayer formulas with the dying person. These may be repeated softly two or three times.

These texts are intended to help the dying person, if still conscious, to face the natural human anxiety about death by imitating Christ in his patient suffering and dying. The Christian will be helped to surmount his or her fear in the hope of heavenly life and resurrection through the power of Christ, who destroyed the power of death by his own dying.

Even if the dying person is not conscious, those who are present will draw consolation from these prayers and come to a better understanding of the paschal character of Christian death. This may be visibly expressed by making the sign of the cross on the forehead of the dying person, who was first signed with the cross at baptism.

Commendation of the Dying

SHORT TEXTS

One or more of the following short texts may be recited with the dying person. If necessary, they may be repeated softly two or three times.

Who can separate us from the love of Christ?	Romans 8:35
Whether we live or die, we are the Lord's.	Romans 14:8
We have an everlasting home in heaven.	2 Corinthians 5:1
We shall be with the Lord for ever.	1 Thessalonians 4:17
We shall see God as he really is.	1 John 3:2
We have passed from death to life because we love each other.	1 John 3:14
To you, Lord, I lift up my soul.	Psalm 24:4
The Lord is my light and my salvation.	Psalm 26:1
I believe that I shall see the goodness of the Lord in the land of the living.	Psalm 26:13
My soul thirsts for the living God.	Psalm 41:3
Though I walk in the shadow of death, I will fear no evil, for you are with me.	Psalm 22:4
Come, blessed of my Father, says the Lord Jesus, and take possession of the kingdom prepared for you.	Matthew 25:34
The Lord Jesus says, today you will be with me in paradise.	Luke 23:43

In my Father's home
there are many dwelling-places,
says the Lord Jesus.   John 14:2

The Lord Jesus says,
I go to prepare a place for you,
and I will come again to take you to myself.   John 14:2-3

I desire that where I am,
they also may be with me,
says the Lord Jesus.   John 17:24

Everyone who believes in the Son
has eternal life.   John 6:40

Into your hands, Lord,
I commend my spirit.   Psalm 30:5

Lord Jesus, receive my spirit.   Acts 7:59

Holy Mary, pray for me.

Saint Joseph, pray for me.

READINGS
Readings may be taken from the Lectionary section of this book (Page 54ff).

SUGGESTED TEXTS:

Job 19:23-27	Page 57
Revelation 21:1-7	Page 64
Matthew 25:1-13	Page 76
Luke 22:39-46	Page 120
Luke 23:44-49	Page 121
Luke 24:1-8	Page 121
John 6:37-40	Page 86
John 14:1-6	Page 91
Psalms 22, 24	Pages 108, 109

LITANY OF THE SAINTS

When the condition of the dying person calls for the use of brief forms of prayer, those who are present are encouraged to pray the litany of the saints – or at least some of its invocations – for him or her. Special mention may be made of the patron saints of the dying person, of the family, and of the parish. The litany may be said or sung in the usual way. Other customary prayers may also be used.

One of the following litanies may be used:

A Lord, have mercy   Lord, have mercy
   Christ, have mercy   Christ, have mercy
   Lord, have mercy   Lord, have mercy

   Holy Mary, Mother of God   pray for him/her
   Holy angels of God   pray for him/her
   Abraham, our father in faith   pray for him/her
   David, leader of God's people   pray for him/her
   All holy patriarchs and prophets   pray for him/her

   Saint John the Baptist   pray for him/her
   Saint Joseph   pray for him/her
   Saint Peter and Saint Paul   pray for him/her
   Saint Andrew   pray for him/her
   Saint John   pray for him/her
   Saint Mary Magdalene   pray for him/her
   Saint Stephen   pray for him/her
   Saint Ignatius   pray for him/her
   Saint Lawrence   pray for him/her
   Saint Perpetua and Saint Felicity   pray for him/her
   Saint Agnes   pray for him/her
   Saint Gregory   pray for him/her
   Saint Augustine   pray for him/her
   Saint Athanasius   pray for him/her
   Saint Basil   pray for him/her
   Saint Martin   pray for him/her
   Saint Benedict   pray for him/her
   Saint Francis and Saint Dominic   pray for him/her
   Saint Francis Xavier   pray for him/her
   Saint John Vianney   pray for him/her
   Saint Catherine   pray for him/her
   Saint Teresa   pray for him/her

Other saints may be included here.

All holy men and women	pray for him/her

Lord, be merciful	Lord, save your people
From all evil	Lord, save your people
From every sin	Lord, save your people
From Satan's power	Lord, save your people
At the moment of death	Lord, save your people
From everlasting death	Lord, save your people
On the day of judgment	Lord, save your people
By your coming as man	Lord, save your people
By your suffering and cross	Lord, save your people
By your death and rising to new life	Lord, save your people
By your return in glory to the Father	Lord, save your people
By your gift of the Holy Spirit	Lord, save your people
By your coming again in glory	Lord, save your people

Be merciful to us sinners	Lord, hear our prayer
Bring N. to eternal life, first promised to him/her in baptism	Lord, hear our prayer
Raise N. on the last day, for he/she has eaten the bread of life	Lord, hear our prayer
Let N. share in your glory, for he/she has shared in your suffering and death	Lord, hear our prayer
Jesus, Son of the living God	Lord, hear our prayer

Christ, hear us	Christ, hear us
Lord Jesus, hear our prayer	Lord Jesus, hear our prayer

B   *A brief form of the litany may be prayed. Other saints may be added, including the patron saints of the dying person, of the family, and of the parish; saints to whom the dying person may have a special devotion may also be included.*

Holy Mary, Mother of God	pray for him/her
Holy angels of God	pray for him/her
Saint John the Baptist	pray for him/her
Saint Peter and Saint Paul	pray for him/her

Other saints may be included here.

All holy men and women	pray for him/her

PRAYER OF COMMENDATION .

When the moment of death seems near, some of the following prayers may be said:

A Go forth, Christian soul, from this world
   in the name of God the almighty Father,
   who created you,
   in the name of Jesus Christ, Son of the living God,
   who suffered for you,
   in the name of the Holy Spirit,
   who was poured out upon you,
   go forth, faithful Christian.

   May you live in peace this day,
   may your home be with God in Zion,
   with Mary, the virgin Mother of God,
   with Joseph, and all the angels and saints.

B I commend you, my dear brother/sister,
   to almighty God,
   and entrust you to your Creator.
   May you return to him
   who formed you from the dust of the earth.
   May holy Mary, the angels, and all the saints
   come to meet you as you go forth from this life.
   May Christ who was crucified for you
   bring you freedom and peace.
   May Christ who died for you
   admit you into his garden of paradise.
   May Christ, the true Shepherd,
   acknowledge you as one of his flock.
   May he forgive all your sins,
   and set you among those he has chosen.
   May you see your Redeemer face to face,
   and enjoy the vision of God for ever.

   R⁷. Amen.

C Welcome your servant, Lord, into the place of salvation
which because of your mercy he/she rightly hoped for.

R⁷. Amen, or R⁷. Lord, save your people.

Deliver your servant, Lord, from every distress. R⁷.

Deliver your servant, Lord, as you delivered Noah from the flood. R⁷.

Deliver your servant, Lord, as you delivered Abraham from Ur of
the Chaldees. R⁷.

Deliver your servant, Lord, as you delivered Job from his sufferings. R⁷.

Deliver your servant, Lord, as you delivered Moses from the hand of
the Pharaoh. R⁷.

Deliver your servant, Lord, as you delivered Daniel from the den of
lions. R⁷.

Deliver your servant, Lord, as you delivered the three young men
from the fiery furnace. R⁷.

Deliver your servant, Lord, as you delivered Susanna from her false
accusers. R⁷.

Deliver your servant, Lord, as you delivered David from the attacks of
Saul and Goliath. R⁷.

Deliver your servant, Lord, as you delivered Peter and Paul from
prison. R⁷.

Deliver your servant, Lord, through Jesus our Saviour, who suffered
death for us and gave us eternal life. R⁷.

D Lord Jesus Christ, Saviour of the world, we pray for your servant N.,
and commend him/her to your mercy.
For his/her sake you came down from heaven;
receive him/her now into the joy of your kingdom.

For though he/she has sinned,
he/she has not denied the Father, the Son,
and the Holy Spirit,
but has believed in God and has worshipped his/her Creator.

R⁷. Amen.

E The following antiphon may be said or sung:

Hail, holy Queen, Mother of mercy, hail, our life, our sweetness, and our hope. To you we cry, the children of Eve; to you we send up our sighs, mourning and weeping in this land of exile. Turn, then, most gracious advocate, your eyes of mercy towards us; lead us home at last and show us the blessed fruit of your womb, Jesus: O clement, O loving, O sweet Virgin Mary.

F Coimirce ár n-anama ort,
   a Rí Mhór na glóire
   ag dul amach dúinn
   is ag teacht isteach,
   ag imeacht dúinn
   is ag filleadh.
   (*Ár bPaidreacha Dúchais*, 175)

G Tabhair dúinn, a Shlánaitheoir áigh,
   eagla Dé, gaol Dé agus grá,
   is toil Dé a dhéanamh ar talamh gach ré
   mar a dhéanann a aingil is a naoimh ar neamh.
   Gach lá is oíche tabhair dúinn do shéimhe.
   (*Ár bPaidreacha Dúchais*, 351)

H Ag Críost an síol,
   ag Críost an fómhar,
   in iothlann Dé go dtugtar sinn.

Ag Críost an mhuir,
ag Críost an t-iasc,
i líonta Dé go gcastar sinn.

Ó fhás go haois
is ó aois go bás
do dhá láimh, a Chríost, anall tharainn.

Ó bhás go críoch
nach críoch ach athfhás,
i bParthas na ngrás go rabhaimid.
(*Ár bPaidreacha Dúchais*, 380)

I Faoi do dhíon, a Rí, do shín do ghéaga ar chrois
   is d'fhulaing tríot na mílte céadta lot,
   luímse síos faoi dhíon do scéithe anocht;
   i mo thimpeall fíor an chrainn do chéas do Chorp.
   (*Ár bPaidreacha Dúchais*, 300)

J A Mhuire na nGrás,
   a Mháthair Mhic Dé,
   go gcuire tú
   ar mo leas mé.

   Go sábhála tú mé
   ar gach uile olc,
   go sábhála tú mé
   idir anam is chorp.

   Go sábhála tú mé
   ar muir is ar tír,
   go sábhála tú mé
   ar lic na bpian.

   Garda na n-aingeal
   os mo chionn,
   Dia romham
   agus Dia liom.
   (*Ár bPaidreacha Dúchais*, 468)

Prayer Immediately after Death

Immediately after death has occurred, all may kneel while one of those present leads the following prayers:

A   Saints of God, come to his/her aid!
    Come to meet him/her, angels of the Lord!

    R7. Receive his/her soul and present him/her to God the Most High.

    May Christ, who called you, take you to himself; may angels lead
    you to Abraham's side. R7.

    Give him/her eternal rest, O Lord, and may your light shine on
    him/her for ever.R7.

    The following prayer is added:

    Let us pray.
    All-powerful and merciful God, we commend to you N., your servant. In your mercy and love, blot out the sins he/she has committed through human weakness. In this world he/she has died: let him/her live with you for ever.

    We ask this through Christ our Lord.
    R7. Amen.

B   Psalm 129   Page 115
    R7. My soul hopes in the Lord.

    The following prayer is added:

    Let us pray.
    God of love, welcome into your presence your son/daughter N.,
    whom you have called from this life. Release him/her from all his/her

sins, bless him/her with eternal light and peace, raise him/her up to
live for ever with all your saints in the glory of the resurrection.

We ask this through Christ our Lord.
R7. Amen.

C Psalm 22   Page 108

R7. Lord, remember me in your kingdom.

The following prayer is added:

Let us pray.
God of mercy, hear our prayers and be merciful to your son/daughter
N., whom you have called from this life. Welcome him/her into the
company of your saints, in the kingdom of light and peace.

We ask this through Christ our Lord.
R7. Amen.

D Almighty and eternal God,
   hear our prayers for your son/daughter N.,
   whom you have called from this life to yourself.

   Grant him/her light, happiness, and peace.
   Let him/her pass in safety through the gates of death,
   and live for ever with all your saints
   in the light you promised to Abraham
   and to all his descendants in faith.

   Guard him/her from all harm
   and on that great day of resurrection and reward
   raise him/her up with all your saints.
   Pardon his/her sins
   and give him/her eternal life in your kingdom.

   We ask this through Christ our Lord.
   R7. Amen.

E Loving and merciful God,
   we entrust our brother/sister to your mercy.

You loved him/her greatly in this life:
now that he/she is freed from all its cares,
give him/her happiness and peace for ever.

The old order has passed away:
welcome him/her now into paradise
where there will be no more sorrow,
no more weeping or pain,
but only peace and joy
with Jesus, your Son,
and the Holy Spirit
for ever and ever.
R⁷. Amen.

F God of our destiny,
   into your hands we commend our brother/sister.
   We are confident that with all who have died in Christ
   he/she will be raised to life on the last day
   and live with Christ for ever.
   [We thank you for all the blessings
   you gave him/her in this life
   to show your fatherly care for all of us
   and the fellowship which is ours with the saints
   in Jesus Christ.]

   Lord, hear our prayer:
   welcome our brother/sister to paradise
   and help us to comfort each other
   with the assurance of our faith
   until we all meet in Christ
   to be with you and with our brother/sister for ever.

   We ask this through Christ our Lord.
   R⁷. Amen.

G Coróin na Marbh
   Ar na clocha móra:
   A Mhaighdean bhráidgheal bhán
   ar daoradh do Mhac sa pháis,
   cuir d'achainí chun Rí na ngrást,
   maithiúnas a thabhairt dó/di is do chách
   is do gach n-aon eile atá ina ghá.

Ar na mionchlocha:
A Íosa Críost, Rí na truamhéala,
suaimhneas síoraí tabhair dóibh, a Thiarna.
Amen.

In áit Glóir don Athair:
Go soilsí solas síoraí dó/di.
(*Ár bPaidreacha Dúchais,* 342)

F. Go gcónaí sé/sí sa tsíocháin
trí thoradh do dhaorpháise.
Amen. Amen, a Íosa.

H Codladh na seacht solas duit, a rún,
codladh na seacht sonas duit, a rún,
codladh na seacht gcodladh duit, a rún,
i mbaclainn Íosa na mbeannacht,
i mbaclainn Íosa na mbua.
(*Carmina Gadelica,* 3, 382)

I Go gcuire Dia an tAthair fáilte romhat:
F. Agus na múrtha fáilte romhat.

Go gcuire Dia an Mac fáilte romhat: F.
Go gcuire Dia an Spiorad Naomh fáilte romhat: F.
Go gcuire Muire, Máthair Dé, fáilte romhat: F.
Go gcuire Mícheál Ardaingeal fáilte romhat: F.
Go gcuire sluaite na nAingeal fáilte romhat: F.
Go gcuire NaomhAithreacha an tSeantiomna fáilte romhat: F.
Go gcuire na Fáithe a réamhfhoilsigh an Slánaitheoir fáilte romhat: F.
Go gcuire Eoin Baiste an réamhtheachtaire fáilte romhat: F.
Go gcuire an dá Aspal déag fáilte romhat: F.
Go gcuire na ceithre Soiscéalaithe fáilte romhat: F.
Go gcuire na Mairtírigh Naofa fáilte romhat: F.
Go gcuire na Coinfeasóirí Naofa fáilte romhat: F.
Go gcuire na Maighdeana Naofa fáilte romhat: F.
Go gcuire na Díthreabhaigh Naofa fáilte romhat: F.
Go gcuire na Manaigh Naofa fáilte romhat: F.
Go gcuire na Cléirigh Naofa fáilte romhat: F.
Go gcuire na Tuataí Naofa fáilte romhat: F.
Go gcuire na Baintreacha Naofa fáilte romhat: F.

Go gcuire na Tiarnaí Naofa fáilte romhat: *F*
Go gcuire na Giollaí Naofa fáilte romhat: *F*
Go gcuire na Saibhre Naofa fáilte romhat: *F*
Go gcuire na Daibhre Naofa fáilte romhat: *F*
Go gcuire Pádraig, Aspal Éireann, fáilte romhat: *F*
Go gcuire Bríd, Muire na nGael, fáilte romhat: *F*
Go gcuire Colm Cille Naofa fáilte romhat: *F*
Go gcuire A. (Pátrún na háite) fáilte romhat: *F*
Go gcuire na Naoimh Uile fáilte romhat: *F*
(*Ár bPaidreacha Dúchais,* 82, 339; *Orthaí Cosanta sa Chráifeacht Cheilteach,* 196)

Prayer for the Family and Friends

One of the following prayers may be said:

Let us pray.
A *For the family and friends*

God of all consolation,
in your unending love and mercy for us
you turn the darkness of death
into the dawn of new life.
Show compassion to your people in their sorrow.

[Be our refuge and our strength
to lift us from the darkness of this grief
to the peace and light of your presence.]

Your Son, our Lord Jesus Christ,
by dying for us, conquered death
and by rising again restored life.

May we then go forward eagerly to meet him,
and after our life on earth
be reunited with our brothers and sisters
where every tear will be wiped away.

We ask this through Christ our Lord.
R7. Amen.

B *For the deceased person and for the family and friends*

Lord Jesus, our Redeemer,
you willingly gave yourself up to death

so that all people might be saved
and pass from death into new life.
Listen to our prayers,
look with love on your people
who mourn and pray for their brother/sister N.

Lord Jesus, holy and compassionate:
forgive N. his/her sins.
By dying you opened the gates of life
for those who believe in you:
do not let our brother/sister be parted from you,
but by your glorious power
give him/her light, joy, and peace in heaven
where you live for ever and ever.
R℣. Amen.

C Go rabhaimid go léir aontaithe lena chéile i ríocht na bhflaitheas –
san áit ina bhfuil
beatha gan bhás,
sláinte gan ghalar,
saoirse gan daoirse,
sonas gan donas
agus an uilemhaitheas i measc na naomh
ar feadh na síoraíochta.
F. Amen
(*Trí Bíor-Ghaoithe an Bháis*, 338)

Prayers for the Dead

The time immediately following death is often one of bewilderment and may involve shock or heart-rending grief for the family and close friends. The ministry of the Church at this time is one of gently accompanying the mourners in their initial adjustment to the fact of death and to the sorrow this entails. The members of the Christian community also offer support to the mourners.

PRAYERS AFTER DEATH
This rite provides a model of prayer that may be used when the minister first meets with the family following death. If the minister has been present with the family at the time of death this rite follows on from the prayers given in *The Pastoral Care of the Sick*, and can be a quiet and prayerful response to the death.

GREETING
The minister greets those who are present, offering them sympathy and the consolation of faith, using one of the following or similar words:

A In this moment of sorrow
   the Lord is in our midst
   and comforts us with his word:
   Blessed are the sorrowful; they shall be consoled.

B Praised be God, the Father of our Lord Jesus Christ,
   the Father of mercies,
   and the God of all consolation!
   He comforts us in all our afflictions
   and thus enables us to comfort those who are in trouble,
   with the same consolation
   we have received from him.

PRAYER
The minister then says one of the following prayers, commending the person
who has just died to God's mercy and goodness:

Let us pray.

A Almighty and eternal God,
 hear our prayers for your son/daughter N.,
 whom you have called from this life to yourself.

 Grant him/her light, happiness, and peace.
 Let him/her pass in safety through the gates of death,
 and live for ever with all your saints
 in the light you promised to Abraham
 and to all his descendants in faith.

 Guard him/her from all harm
 and on that great day of resurrection and reward
 raise him/her up with all your saints.
 Pardon his/her sins
 and give him/her eternal life in your kingdom.
 We ask this through Christ our Lord.
 R7. Amen.

B Loving and merciful God,
 we entrust our brother/sister to your mercy.

 You loved him/her greatly in this life:
 now that he/she is freed from all its cares,
 give him/her happiness and peace for ever.

 The old order has passed away:
 welcome him/her now into paradise
 where there will be no more sorrow,
 no more weeping or pain,
 but only peace and joy
 with Jesus, your Son,
 and the Holy Spirit
 for ever and ever.
 R7. Amen.

READING

The word of God is proclaimed by one of those present or by the minister. An appropriate reading from the Funeral Lectionary or one of the following readings may be used:

A A reading from the holy Gospel according to Luke 23:44-49
   Page 121

B A reading from the holy Gospel according to John 11:3-7.17.20-
   27.33-35.41b-44 Page 122

LITANY

Then one of those present may lead the others in praying a brief form of the litany of the saints. (The full form of the litany of the saints may be found on pages 6-7.) Other saints may be added, including the patron saints of the dead person, of the family, and of the parish; saints to whom the deceased person may have had a special devotion may also be included.

Saints of God, come to his/her aid!
Come to meet him/her, angels of the Lord!

Holy Mary, Mother of God	pray for him/her
Saint Joseph	pray for him/her
Saint Peter and Saint Paul	pray for him/her

The following prayer is added:

God of mercy,
hear our prayers and be merciful
to your son/daughter N., whom you have called
from this life.
Welcome him/her into the company of your saints,
in the kingdom of light and peace.

We ask this through Christ our Lord.

R7. Amen.

THE LORD'S PRAYER
The minister introduces the Lord's Prayer in these or similar words:

A With God there is mercy and fullness of redemption;
   let us pray as Jesus taught us to pray:

B Let us pray for the coming of the kingdom as Jesus taught us:

All:

Our Father . . .

PRAYER OF COMMENDATION
The minister then concludes with the following prayer:

> Lord Jesus, our Redeemer,
> you willingly gave yourself up to death
> so that all people might be saved
> and pass from death into a new life.
> Listen to our prayers,
> look with love on your people
> who mourn and pray for their brother/sister N.
>
> Lord Jesus, holy and compassionate:
> forgive N. his/her sins.
> By dying you opened the gates of life
> for those who believe in you:
> do not let our brother/sister be parted from you,
> but by your glorious power
> give him/her light, joy, and peace in heaven
> where you live for ever and ever.
>
> R7. Amen.

For the solace of those present the minister may conclude these prayers with a simple blessing or with a symbolic gesture, for example, signing the forehead with the sign of the cross. A priest or deacon may sprinkle the body with holy water.

Gathering in the Presence of the Body

If we died with Christ, we believe we shall also live with him.

This rite provides a model of prayer that may be used when the family first gathers in the presence of the body, when the body is to be prepared for burial, or after it has been prepared. The family members, in assembling in the presence of the body, confront in the most immediate way the fact of their loss and the mystery of death.

Through the presence of the minister and others and through the celebration of this brief rite, the community seeks to be with the mourners in their need and to provide an atmosphere of sensitive concern and confident faith. In prayer and gesture those present show reverence for the body of the deceased as a temple of the life-giving Spirit and ask, in that same Spirit, for the eternal life promised to the faithful.

The minister should try to be as attentive as possible to the particular needs of the mourners. The minister begins the rite at an opportune moment and, as much as possible, in an atmosphere of calm and recollection. The pause for silent prayer after the Scripture verse can be especially helpful in this regard. Because cultural attitudes and practices on such occasions may vary, the minister should adapt the rite.

SIGN OF THE CROSS
The minister and those present sign themselves with the sign of the cross as the minister says:

In the name of the Father, and of the Son, and of the Holy Spirit.

R⁊. Amen.

SCRIPTURE VERSE
One of the following or another brief Scripture verse is read.

A Matthew 11:28-30

My brothers and sisters, Jesus says: 'Come to me, all you who labour and are overburdened, and I will give you rest. Shoulder my yoke and learn from me, for I am gentle and humble in heart, and you will find rest for your souls. Yes, my yoke is easy and my burden light.'

B John 14:1-3

My brothers and sisters, Jesus says:
'Do not let your hearts be troubled.
Trust in God still and trust in me.
There are many rooms in my Father's house;
if there were not, I should have told you.
I am going now to prepare a place for you,
and after I have gone and prepared you a place,
I shall return to take you with me,
so that where I am
you may be too.'

SPRINKLING WITH HOLY WATER
Using one of the following formularies, the minister may sprinkle the body with holy water.

A The Lord is our shepherd
   and leads us to streams of living water.

B Let this water call to mind our baptism into Christ,
   who by his death and resurrection has redeemed us.

C The Lord God lives in his holy temple yet abides in our midst.
   Since in baptism N. became God's temple
   and the Spirit of God lived in him/her,
   with reverence we bless his/her mortal body.

PSALM
One of the following psalms or another psalm is sung or said.

A R7. I hope in the Lord, I trust in his word.
   Psalm 129 Page 115

B R7. I will walk in the presence of the Lord, in the land of the living.
   Psalm 114/115 Pages 113-4 (Cited as Pss 114 &115)

THE LORD'S PRAYER
Using one of the following invitations, or in similar words, the minister invites those present to pray the Lord's Prayer.

A With God there is mercy and fullness of redemption;
   let us pray as Jesus taught us:

B Let us pray for the coming of the kingdom as Jesus taught us:

   All:
   Our Father . . .

CONCLUDING PRAYER
The minister says one of the following prayers or one of those provided in the Order of Christian Funerals.

A God of faithfulness,
   in your wisdom you have called your servant N.
   out of this world;
   release him/her from the bonds of sin,
   and welcome him/her into your presence,
   so that he/she may enjoy eternal light and peace
   and be raised up in glory with all our saints.
   We ask this through Christ our Lord.
   R7. Amen.

B Into your hands, O Lord,
   we humbly entrust our brother/sister N.
   In this life you embraced him/her with your tender love;
   deliver him/her now from every evil
   and bid him/her enter eternal rest.
   The old order has passed away:

Welcome him/her then into paradise,
where there will be no sorrow, no weeping nor pain,
but the fullness of peace and joy
with your Son and the Holy Spirit
for ever and ever.

R̷. Amen.

BLESSING
The minister says:

Blessed are those who have died in the Lord;

let them rest from their labours for their good deeds go with them.

A gesture, for example, signing the forehead of the deceased with the sign of the cross, may accompany the following words.

Eternal rest grant unto him/her, O Lord.
R̷. And let perpetual light shine upon him/her.

May he/she rest in peace.
R̷. Amen.

May his/her soul and the souls of all the faithful departed, through the mercy of God, rest in peace.
R̷. Amen.

A *A minister who is a priest or deacon says:*

May the peace of God,
which is beyond all understanding,
keep your hearts and minds
in the knowledge and love of God
and of his Son, our Lord Jesus Christ.
R̷. Amen.

May almighty God bless you,
the Father, and the Son, ✠ and the Holy Spirit.
R̷. Amen.

B *A lay minister invokes God's blessing and signs himself or herself with the sign of the cross, saying:*

May the love of God and the peace of the Lord Jesus Christ
bless and console us
and gently wipe every tear from our eyes:
in the name of the Father,
and of the Son, and of the Holy Spirit.
R7. Amen.

Vigil for the Deceased

Happy now are the dead who die in the Lord;
they shall find rest from their labours.

The vigil for the deceased is the principal rite celebrated by the Christian community in the time following death and before the funeral liturgy or, if there is no funeral liturgy, before the rite of committal.

It is particularly suitable for celebration during the wake and may be led by a lay minister. The ministry of gathering the believing Church around the bereaved is the responsibility of the ordained, yet the *Order of Christian Funerals* provides for those times when lay people share that ministry and recognises that it may often fall to the funeral director to fulfil other roles besides caring for the business of the funeral.

The vigil may be celebrated in the home of the deceased, in the funeral home, in the mortuary chapel, or in some other suitable place. It may also be celebrated in the church, but at a time well before the funeral liturgy, so that the funeral liturgy will not be lengthy nor the liturgy of the word repetitious. Adaptations of the vigil will often be suggested by the place in which the celebration occurs. A celebration in the home of the deceased, for example, may be simplified and shortened.

The vigil may also take the form of Morning Prayer or Evening Prayer from the Office for the Dead.

This vigil is seen as a valuable moment of prayer with the bereaved for the deceased. There is more substance than merely viewing the body and saying a personal prayer while expressing sympathy. The vigil service educates people of faith about the values of the funeral liturgy and the faith of the Catholic and Christian community. Such education leads to greater participation. Pastoral practice requires sensitivity to the wishes of the deceased and the family. There is sufficient time during the wake for group devotions. Some forms of the Rosary, including meditations on the Glorious Mysteries, have been created for funeral situations.

At the vigil the Christian community keeps watch with the family in prayer to the God of mercy and finds strength in Christ's presence. It is the first occasion among the funeral rites for the solemn reading of the word of God. In this time of loss the family and community turn to God's word as the source of faith and hope, as light and life in the face of darkness and death. Consoled by the redeeming word of God and by the abiding presence of Christ and Spirit, the assembly at the vigil calls upon the Father of mercy to receive the deceased into the kingdom of light and peace.

STRUCTURE
The vigil, in the form of the liturgy of the word, consists of the introductory rites, the liturgy of the word, the prayer of intercession, and a concluding rite.

INTRODUCTORY RITES
The introductory rites gather the faithful together to form a community and prepare all to listen to God's word. The introductory rites of the vigil for the deceased include the greeting, an opening song, an invitation to prayer, a pause for silent prayer, and an opening prayer.

The opening song or entrance song should be a profound expression of belief in eternal life and the resurrection of the dead, as well as a prayer of intercession for the dead.

LITURGY OF THE WORD
The proclamation of the word of God is the high point and central focus of the vigil. The liturgy of the word usually includes a first reading, responsorial psalm, gospel reading and homily. A reader proclaims the first reading. The responsorial psalm should be sung whenever possible. If an assisting deacon is present, he proclaims the gospel reading. Otherwise it is proclaimed by the presiding minister.

The purpose of the readings at the vigil is to proclaim the paschal mystery, teach remembrance of the dead, convey the hope of being gathered together in God's kingdom, and encourage the witness of Christian life. Above all, the readings tell of God's designs for a world in which suffering and death will relinquish their hold on all whom God has called his own. The responsorial psalm enables the community to respond in faith to the reading and to express its grief and its praise of God. In the selection of readings the needs of the mourners and the circumstances of the death should be kept in mind.

A homily based on the readings may be given at the vigil to help those present to find strength and hope in God's saving word.

PRAYER OF INTERCESSION

In the prayer of intercession the community calls upon God to comfort the mourners and to show mercy to the deceased. The prayer of intercession takes the form of a litany, the Lord's Prayer, and a concluding prayer.

After this prayer and before the blessing, or at some other suitable time during the vigil, a member of the family or a friend of the deceased may speak in remembrance of the deceased.

CONCLUDING RITE

The vigil concludes with a blessing, which may be followed by a liturgical song, or a few moments of silent prayer, or both.

MINISTRY AND PARTICIPATION

Members of the local parish community should be encouraged to participate in the vigil as a sign of concern and support for the mourners. In many circumstances the vigil will be the first opportunity for friends, neighbours, and members of the local parish community to show their concern for the family of the deceased by gathering for prayer. The vigil may also serve as an opportunity for participation in the funeral by those who, because of work or other reasons, cannot be present for the funeral liturgy or the rite of committal.

The full participation by all present is to be encouraged. This is best achieved through careful planning of the celebration. Whenever possible, the family of the deceased should take part in the selection of texts and music and in the designation of liturgical ministers.

Besides the presiding minister, other available ministers (a reader, a cantor, an acolyte) should exercise their ministries. Family members may assume some of these liturgical roles, unless their grief prevents them from doing so.

The presiding minister and assisting ministers should vest for the vigil according to local custom. If the vigil is celebrated in the church, a priest or deacon who presides wears an alb or surplice with stole.

As needs require, and especially if the funeral liturgy or rite of committal is not to take place for a few days, the vigil may be celebrated more than once and should be adapted to each occasion.

Music is integral to any vigil, especially the vigil for the deceased. In the difficult circumstances following death, well-chosen music can touch the mourners and others present at levels of human need that words alone often fail to reach. Such music can enliven the faith of the community gathered to support the family and to affirm hope in the resurrection.

Whenever possible, an instrumentalist and a cantor or leader of song should assist the assembly's full participation in the singing.

In the choice of music for the vigil, preference should be given to the singing of the opening song and the responsorial psalm. The litany, the Lord's Prayer, and a closing song may also be sung.

Outline of the Rite

Introductory Rites

> Sign of the Cross
> Greeting
> Opening Song
> Invitation to Prayer
> Opening Prayer

Liturgy of the Word

> First Reading
> Responsorial Psalm
> Gospel
> Homily

Prayer of Intercession

> Litany
> The Lord's Prayer
> Concluding Prayer

Concluding Rite

> Blessing

Introductory Rites

SIGN OF THE CROSS
The minister and those present sign themselves with the sign of the cross as the minister says:

In the name of the Father, and of the Son, and of the Holy Spirit.

R⁷. Amen.

GREETING
Using one of the following greetings, or in similar words, the minister greets those present.

A May the God of hope give you the fullness of peace, and may the Lord of life be always with you.

R⁷. And also with you.

B The grace and peace of God our Father and the Lord Jesus Christ be with you.

R⁷. And also with you.

C The grace and peace of God our Father, who raised Jesus from the dead, be always with you.

R⁷. And also with you.

D May the Father of mercies, the God of all consolation, be with you.

R⁷. And also with you.

OPENING SONG
The celebration continues with a song.

INVITATION TO PRAYER
In the following or similar words, the minister invites those present to pray.

My brothers and sisters, we believe that all the ties of friendship and affection which knit us as one throughout our lives do not unravel with death.

Confident that God always remembers the good we have done and forgives our sins, let us pray, asking God to gather N. to himself:

Pause for silent prayer.

OPENING PRAYER
The minister says one of the following prayers or one of those provided in the Order of Christian Funerals.

A Lord our God, the death of our brother/sister N.
   recalls our human condition
   and the brevity of our lives on earth.
   But for those who believe in your love
   death is not the end,
   nor does it destroy the bonds
   that you forged in our lives.
   We share the faith of your Son's disciples
   and the hope of the children of God.
   Bring the light of Christ's resurrection
   to this time of testing and pain
   as we pray for N. and for those who love him/her,
   through Christ our Lord.
   R7. Amen.

B O God,
   glory of believers and life of the just,
   by the death and resurrection of your Son, we are
   redeemed:
   have mercy on your servant N.,
   and make him/her worthy to share the joys of paradise,
   for he/she believed in the resurrection of the dead.

   We ask this through Christ our Lord.
   R7. Amen.

Liturgy of the Word
The celebration continues with the liturgy of the word.

The following or other readings, psalms and gospel readings may be chosen from the Funeral Lectionary.

FIRST READING

A reading from the second letter of Paul to the Corinthians 5:1.6-10
Page 70

We have an everlasting home in heaven.

RESPONSORIAL PSALM
The following psalm or another psalm or song is sung or said.

R7. The Lord is my light and my salvation.

or

R7. I believe that I shall see the good things of the Lord in the land of the
    living. Psalm 26 Pages 109-110

GOSPEL
A reading from the holy Gospel according to Luke 12:35-40 Page 80

Be prepared.

Prayer of Intercession

LITANY
The minister leads those present in the following litany.

Let us turn to Christ Jesus with confidence and faith in the power of his
cross and resurrection:

> *Assisting minister:*
> Risen Lord, pattern of our life for ever:
> Lord, have mercy.
> R7. Lord, have mercy.

Assisting minister:
Promise and image of what we shall be:
Lord, have mercy.
R7. Lord, have mercy.

Assisting minister:
Son of God, who came to destroy sin and death:
Lord, have mercy.
R7. Lord, have mercy.

Assisting minister:
Word of God, who delivered us from the fear of death:
Lord, have mercy.
R7. Lord, have mercy.

Assisting minister:
Crucified Lord, forsaken in death, raised in glory:
Lord, have mercy.
R7. Lord, have mercy.

Assisting minister:
Lord Jesus, gentle Shepherd who brings rest to our souls,
give peace to N. for ever:
Lord, have mercy.
R7. Lord, have mercy.

Assisting minister:
Lord Jesus, you bless those who mourn and are in pain. Bless
N.'s family and friends who gather around him/her today:
Lord, have mercy.
R7. Lord, have mercy.

THE LORD'S PRAYER
Using one of the following invitations, or in similar words, the minister invites those present to pray the Lord's Prayer.

A Friends [Brothers and sisters], our true home is heaven.
   Therefore let us pray to our heavenly Father as Jesus taught us:

B With God there is mercy and fullness of redemption; let us pray as
   Jesus taught us:

C Let us pray for the coming of the Kingdom as Jesus taught us:

> *All:*
> Our Father . . .

CONCLUDING PRAYER
The minister says one of the following prayers or one of those provided in nos. 314-315.

A Lord Jesus our Redeemer,
    you willingly gave yourself up to death,
    so that all might be saved and pass from death to life.
    We humbly ask you to comfort your servants in their grief
    and to receive N. into the arms of your mercy.
    You alone are the Holy One,
    you are mercy itself;
    by dying you unlocked the gates of life
    for those who believe in you.
    Forgive N. his/her sins,
    and grant him/her a place of happiness, light, and peace
    in the kingdom of your glory for ever.

   R7. Amen.

B Lord God,
    You are attentive to the voice of our pleading.
    Let us find in your Son
    comfort in our sadness,
    certainty in our doubt,
    and courage to live through this hour.
    Make our faith strong
    through Christ our Lord.

   R7. Amen.

Concluding Rite

BLESSING

The minister says:

Blessed are those who have died in the Lord;
let them rest from their labours for their good deeds go with them.

A gesture, for example, signing the forehead of the deceased with the sign of the cross, or sprinkling with holy water, may accompany the following words.

Eternal rest grant unto him/her, O Lord.
R⁊. And let perpetual light shine upon him/her.

May he/she rest in peace.
R⁊. Amen.

May his/her soul and the souls of all the faithful departed,
through the mercy of God, rest in peace.
R⁊. Amen.

A *A minister who is a priest or deacon says:*

May almighty God bless you,
the Father, and the Son, ✠ and the Holy Spirit.
R⁊. Amen.

B *A lay minister invokes God's blessing and signs himself or herself with the sign of the cross, saying:*

May the love of God and the peace of the Lord Jesus Christ
bless and console us
and gently wipe every tear from our eyes:
in the name of the Father,
and of the Son, and of the Holy Spirit.
R⁊. Amen.

The vigil may conclude with a song, or a few moments of silent prayer, or both.

The Rosary may be recited.

Transfer of the Body to the Church

This short rite is to be used at the gathering of the family, close friends and mourners for the removal of the body from the home, funeral home or mortuary chapel to the church. While the rite is short it should not be rushed. Local custom regarding the Rosary may be retained.

It is presumed that generally the body will already have been placed in the coffin, and that the rite will be celebrated immediately before the sealing of the coffin. The rite includes prayers for the private use of members of the family. (Although these prayers are placed at the end of the rite, they can be used at other times as required.) The moment of the sealing of the coffin is an emotional one for the immediate family. It should be approached with sensitivity, and privacy should be ensured. The family may wish to say a final farewell, and to do so in their own personal way – a kiss, a touch, signing on the forehead or sprinkling with holy water.

The rite includes a choice of scripture verses. Others may also be used, while avoiding what will later be used during the liturgy of the word at the reception at the church.

Ideally the coffin is brought in procession from the home, funeral home or mortuary chapel to the church. This is most evident on those rare occasions when, following tradition, the coffin is carried to the church accompanied by the family and friends walking in procession. Particularly in urban contexts, in which mourners travel by motor vehicles, it is difficult to create this sense of procession. However, it is possible to preserve a sense of this tradition if the minister leads the gathered mourners in suitable prayers (such as the Rosary or Litany of the Saints) while the family accompany the coffin to the waiting hearse to begin the journey to the church.

This rite of removal will frequently be led by a lay person, either a member of the family or a minister designated by the local community.

Outline of the Rite

> Sign of the Cross
> Invitation
> Scripture Verse
> Litany
> The Lord's Prayer
> Concluding Prayer
> Invitation to the Procession
> Family Private Farewell
> Removal of the Coffin and Procession to the Church

Transfer of the Body to the Church

SIGN OF THE CROSS
The minister and those present sign themselves with the sign of the cross as the minister says:

In the name of the Father, and of the Son, and of the Holy Spirit.

R7. Amen.

INVITATION
Dear friends in Christ, in the name of Jesus and of his Church, we gather to pray for N., that God may bring him/her to everlasting peace and rest.

We share the pain of loss, but the promise of eternal life gives us hope. Let us comfort one another with these words:

SCRIPTURE VERSE

One of the following or another brief Scripture verse is read.

A Romans 6:8-9 (RSV)

> If we have died with Christ, we believe that we shall also live with him. For we know that Christ, being raised from the dead, will never die again; death no longer has dominion over him.

B Colossians 3:3-4

You have died, and now the life you have is hidden with Christ in God. But when Christ is revealed – and he is your life – you too will be revealed in all your glory with him.

LITANY
The minister leads those present in the following litany.

Dear friends, our Lord comes to raise the dead and comforts us with the solace of his love. Let us praise the Lord Jesus Christ.

Assisting minister:
Word of God, Creator of the earth to which N. now returns; in baptism you called him/her to eternal life to praise your Father for ever: Lord, have mercy.

R7. Lord, have mercy.

Assisting minister:
Son of God, you raise up the just and clothe them with the glory of your kingdom:
Lord, have mercy.

R7. Lord, have mercy.

Assisting minister:
Crucified Lord, you protect the soul of N. by the power of your cross, and on the day of your coming you will show mercy to all the faithful departed:
Lord, have mercy.

R7. Lord, have mercy.

Assisting minister:
Judge of the living and the dead, at your voice the tombs will open and all the just who sleep in your peace will rise and sing the glory of God: Lord, have mercy.

R7. Lord, have mercy.

Assisting minister:
All praise to you, Jesus our Saviour, death is in your hands and all the living depend on you alone:
Lord, have mercy.

R7. Lord, have mercy.

THE LORD'S PRAYER
In the following or similar words, the minister invites those present to pray the Lord's Prayer.

With faith and hope we pray to the Father in the words Jesus taught his disciples:

All:

Our Father . . .

CONCLUDING PRAYER
The minister says one of the following prayers or one of those provided in the appendix.

A Lord,
   N. is gone now from this earthly dwelling and has left behind those who mourn his/her absence. Grant that as we grieve for our brother/sister, we may hold his/her memory dear and live in hope of the eternal kingdom where you will bring us together again.
   We ask this through Christ our Lord.

R7. Amen.

B God of all consolation,
   open our hearts to your word, so that, listening to it, we may comfort one another, finding light in time of darkness and faith in time of doubt.
   We ask this through Christ our Lord.

R7. Amen.

The minister then says the following:

Eternal rest grant unto him/her, O Lord.

R7. And let perpetual light shine upon him/her.

May he/she rest in peace.

R7. Amen.

May his/her soul and the souls of all the faithful departed, through the mercy of God, rest in peace.

R7. Amen.

INVITATION TO THE PROCESSION
In the following or similar words, the minister invites those present to join in the procession.

The Lord guards our coming in and our going out.
May God be with us now as we prepare to accompany our brother/ sister on his/her journey (to the church).

FAMILY PRIVATE FAREWELL
The mourners depart and prepare to accompany the body to the church. The family may wish to remain for a private final farewell. A gesture of farewell (such as touching or sprinkling with holy water) may be made in accordance with local custom.

As the coffin is about to be sealed a prayer such as the following may be said:

May Christ now enfold you in his love and bring you to eternal life.

We will pray for you, N.,
may you pray for us.

May God and Mary be with you.

The coffin is then sealed and removed.

REMOVAL OF THE COFFIN AND PROCESSION TO THE CHURCH

According to local custom or needs the minister may lead the mourners in prayer (such as the Rosary, the Litany of the Saints or Psalms) while the family accompany the removal of the coffin from the home or mortuary chapel.

Other Devotional Prayers and Reflections

These prayers and reflections are not part of the Order of Christian Funerals. The rites allow for additional devotions at the various gatherings in the home, and these texts are given as a help for these situations, not for the rites in the church. The family may suggest other prayers or devotions.

FOR THE DYING

A Soul of Christ sanctify me,
   Body of Christ save me,
   Blood of Christ inebriate me,
   Water from the side of Christ wash me,
   Splendour of the face of Christ illuminate me,
   Passion of Christ strengthen me,
   Sweat from the face of Christ heal me,
   O good Jesus hear me,
   Within thy wounds hide me,
   Suffer me not to be separated from thee,
   From the malicious enemy defend me,
   In the hour of my death call me,
   And bid me come to thee,
   That with thy saints and angels I may praise thee,
   For ever and ever. Amen.

B May he support us all the day long, till the shades lengthen, and the evening comes, and the busy world is hushed, and the fever of life is over, and our work is done. Then in his mercy may he give us a safe lodging, and a holy rest, and peace at the last. (Cardinal Newman)

C O my most blessed and glorious Creator, who has fed me all my life long, and redeemed me from all evil; seeing it is your merciful pleasure to take me out of this frail body, and to wipe away all tears from my eyes, and all sorrows from my heart, I do with all humility and willingness consent and submit myself wholly to your sacred will. My most loving Redeemer, into your saving and everlasting arms I commend my spirit; I am ready, my dear Lord, and earnestly expect and long for your good pleasure. Come quickly and receive the soul of your servant who trusts in you. (Henry Vaughan (1621-1695), adapted)

D God be in my head
   And in my understanding,
   God be in mine eyes
   And in my looking,
   God be in my mouth
   And in my speaking,
   God be in my heart
   And in my thinking,
   God be at mine end
   And at my departing.

E Saint Joseph, pray for us.
   Consolation of those in trouble, pray for us.
   Hope of the sick, pray for us.
   Patron of the dying, pray for us.
   Terror of demons, pray for us.

F My Lord and Saviour, support me in my last hour in the strong arm of your sacraments and by the fresh fragrance of your consolations. Let the absolving words be said over me, and your own body be my food, and your blood my sprinkling; and let my sweet mother, Mary, breathe on me; and my angel whisper peace to me, and my patron saints smile on me; that in them all and through them all, I may receive the gift of perseverance, and die, as I desire to live, in your faith, in your Church, in your service, and in your love. Amen.

G Jesus, Mary, and Joseph,
   I give you my heart and my soul.
   Jesus, Mary and Joseph,
   assist me in my last agony.
   Jesus, Mary and Joseph,
   may I sleep and rest in peace with you.

   Mary, mother of grace, mother of mercy,
   guard me from the enemy,
   and receive me at the hour of death.

H I firmly believe all the articles of faith, and all that the holy, Catholic, and Apostolic Roman Church believes and teaches.

I hope that Christ our Lord in his infinite mercy will take pity on me; and that by the merits of his sacred Passion, and at the intercession of our Lady and all the saints, I may gain eternal life.

I love God with all my heart, and desire that my love for him may be as great as that of all the saints and blessed spirits.

For love of my Lord I grieve with all my heart for the sins of whatever kind I have committed against God, and against my neighbour.

For love of God I sincerely forgive all my enemies, and all who have done me harm. I ask pardon of those I have injured by word and deed.

For God's sake I will bear patiently, as penance for my sins, all the pain and suffering of this illness.

I resolve, if the Lord should graciously spare my life, to keep the commandments with all my strength, and to beware of sinning in future.

AFTER DEATH

A Into thy hands, O most merciful Saviour, we commend the soul of thy servant, now departed from the body.

Acknowledge, we humbly beseech thee, a sheep of thine own fold, a lamb of thine own flock, a sinner of thine own redeeming.

Receive him/her into the arms of thy mercy, into the blessed rest of everlasting peace, and into the glorious company of the saints in light.
(John Cosin [(1596-1672])

B O Jesus, lover of souls, we recommend unto you the souls of all your servants, who have departed with the sign of faith and sleep the sleep of peace. We beseech you, Lord and Saviour, that, as in your mercy to them you became man, so now you would admit them to your presence above.

Gracious Lord, we beseech you, remember not against them the sins of their youth and their ignorance; but be mindful of them in your heavenly glory. May the heavens be opened to them. May the Archangel St Michael conduct them to you. May your holy angels come forth to meet them, and carry them to the city of the heavenly Jerusalem. May they rest in peace.

C We seem to give them back to you, O God, who gave them to us.

Yet as you did not lose them in giving, so we do not lose them by their return.

Not as the world gives, do you give, O lover of souls.
What you give, you do not take away, for what is yours is ours also, if we are yours.
And life is eternal and love is immortal, and death is only an horizon, and an horizon is nothing save the limit of our sight.
Lift us up, strong Son of God, that we may see further; cleanse our eyes that we may see more clearly;
draw us closer to yourself that we may know ourselves to be nearer to our loved ones who are with you.
And while you prepare a place for us, prepare us also for that happy place, that where you are we may be also for ever more. Amen.

D In God we live and move and have our being. Alive or dead, we are all in him. It would be more true to say that we are all alive in him, and that there is no death. Our God is not the God of the dead but of the living. He is your God, the God of her/him who has died. There is only one God, and in this one God you are both united. Only you cannot see each other for the time being. But this means that your future meeting will be the more joyful; and then no one will take your joy from you. Yet even now you live together; all that has happened is that she/he has gone into another room and closed the door.... Spiritual love transcends visible separation.
(S. Tyszkiewicz and T. Belpaire, *A Sourcebook About Christian Death*)

E Lord Jesus, in your life on earth you knew all about partings.
You had to leave your home and family to go into the wider world, to preach the good news.
You had to part company with the establishment of your time;
Lazarus died and you wept;
your closest friends deserted you in your hour of need –
one even betrayed you to your enemies.
But though you knew partings, they did not overwhelm you.
In love you went through their painfulness.
Strengthen me in the pain of the parting I have just undergone. Let me feel your support and know that in some strange way my prayer will be deepened through my pain.
Then, through my experience of your closeness and love,
help me to help others when they are struck by the grief of death and parting.
(Michael Hollings & Etta Gullick, *Prayers Before and After Death*)

F Long ago your servant St Francis
   praised you, O God, for all your creatures.
   For Brother Sun and Sister Moon he sang to you,
   for wind and water, birds and beasts.
   He praised you even for death.
   So be praised, my Lord, for Sister Death,
   most kind and gentle death
   that leads home your son/daughter N.
   In suffering he/she learned how this life is an exile,
   this world a place of tears.
   We give you thanks for the blessing he/she was in our midst.
   May N. now find rest with all your holy ones,
   and with them may he/she sing your praise for ever and ever.
   (Gabe Huck)

Prayer to Accompany the Time of Death of a Child

*Prepared by a subcommittee of the National Liturgy
Commission for Ireland*

Introduction
The following is intended to provide a structure for prayer to accompany
the time of death of a child, that is, the time immediately before death
occurs, the moment of death itself, and the period immediately following
death.

The rite is intended primarily for use with the parents and family in either
the home or hospital setting. It is a simplification of the rite provided for
general purposes.

The elements of the rite are as follows:

APPROACHING DEATH
1. Sign of the Cross
2. Short Texts
   (if time allows or conditions require)
3. Scripture Verse
4. Litany of the Saints
5. Keeping Watch
   THE MOMENT OF DEATH
6. Prayer of Commendation
7. Prayer at the moment of death
   AFTER DEATH
8. Prayer for the deceased
9. Prayer for the family and friends
10. Concluding Prayer

APPROACHING DEATH

A parent or other close friend should hold the child or, if that is not possible, the hand of the child. A member of the family or other person may hold a candle for the dying child.

Sign of the Cross

Short Texts

One or more of the following short texts may be recited with the dying child:

Luke 23:43 He replied, 'Truly I tell you, today you will be with me in Paradise.'

Mark 10:15 'Truly I tell you, whoever does not receive the kingdom of God as a little child will never enter it.'

2 Corinthians 5:1 For we know that if the earthly tent we live in is destroyed, we have a building from God, a house not made with hands, eternal in the heavens.

John 14:2 In my Father's house there are many dwelling places. If it were not so, would I have told you that I go to prepare a place for you?

Matthew 18:4 Whoever becomes humble like this child is the greatest in the kingdom of heaven.

Scripture Verse

If time allows, a selection from the following may be made.

Mark 10:13-16 People were bringing little children to him in order that he might touch them; and the disciples spoke sternly to them. But when Jesus saw this, he was indignant and said to them, 'Let the little children come to me; do not stop them; for it is to such as these that the kingdom of God belongs.' And he took them up in his arms, laid his hands on them, and blessed them.

Matthew 7:9-11 Is there anyone among you who, if your child asks for bread, will give a stone? Or if the child asks for a fish, will give a snake? If you then, who are evil, know how to give good gifts to your children, how much more will your Father in heaven give good things to those who ask him!

John 17:12-16 While I was with them, I protected them in your name that you have given me. I guarded them, and not one of them was lost except the one destined to be lost, so that the scripture might be fulfilled. They do not belong to the world, just as I do not belong to the world.

John 17:23-24 I in them and you in me, that they may become completely one, so that the world may know that you have sent me and have loved them even as you have loved me. Father, I desire that those also, whom you have given me, may be with me where I am, to see my glory, which you have given me because you loved me before the foundation of the world.

Litany of the Saints
Usual form as on Page 6
(Other saints may be included here.)

All holy men and women care for him/her.
You became a little child for our sake, sharing our human life:

   R⁊. Bless us and keep us, O Lord.

You grew in wisdom, age, and grace, and learned obedience through suffering:

   R⁊. Bless us and keep us, O Lord.

You welcomed children, promising them your kingdom:

   R⁊. Bless us and keep us, O Lord.

You took upon yourself the suffering and death of us all:

   R⁊. Bless us and keep us, O Lord.

You promised to raise up those who believe in you, just as you were raised up in glory by the Father:

   R⁊. Bless us and keep us, O Lord.

Keeping Watch
Members of the family and friends may wish to offer a personal farewell to the dying child. If time allows, and conditions permit, those present may continue to support the dying child and each other in quiet prayer. The following are provided as resources.

The Lord is my Shepherd *(Psalm 22) Page 108*

Saint Patrick's Breastplate

Christ be beside me, Christ be before me,
Christ be behind me, King of my heart.
Christ be within me, Christ be below me,
Christ be above me, never to part.

Christ on my right hand, Christ on my left hand,
Christ all around me, shield in the strife,
Christ in my sleeping, Christ in my sitting,
Christ in my rising, Light of my life.

Christ be in all hearts thinking about me,
Christ be on all tongues telling of me.
Christ be the vision in eyes that see me,
In ears that hear me, Christ ever be.

AT THE MOMENT OF DEATH
Prayer of Commendation
When the moment of death seems near, some of the following prayer may be said.

May a procession of angels, a procession of apostles,
a procession of saints come to meet you
and carry your soul to God's right hand.

Prayer at the Moment of Death

Our Father…

Dying you destroyed our Death,
Rising you restored our Life;
Lord Jesus, come in Glory.

Glory be to the Father, and to the Son,
and to the Holy Spirit…

Hail, holy Queen, Mother of mercy…

AFTER DEATH
Prayer for the deceased
N.,
May Christ now enfold you in his love
and bring you to eternal life.
We will pray for you, N.

May you pray for us.
May God and Mary be with you. (111)

Prayer for the family and friends
Lord God,
you are attentive to the voice of our pleading.
Let us find in your Son
comfort in our sadness,
certainty in our doubt,
and courage to live through this hour.
Make our faith strong
through Christ our Lord.
R⁷. Amen.

Concluding prayer
*If a priest or deacon is present they may sprinkle the body with holy water.
Members of the family and friends may wish to sign the forehead of the deceased with the sign of the cross.*

N.,
May the Lord bless you and keep you.
May he let his face shine on you and be gracious to you.
May the Lord show you his face, and bring you peace.

Numbers 6:23

Eternal rest grant unto him/her, O Lord.
R⁷. And let perpetual light shine upon him/her.

May he/she rest in peace.
R⁷. Amen.

May his/her soul and the souls of all the faithful departed,
through the mercy of God, rest in peace.
R⁷. Amen.

The Funeral Readings

INTRODUCTION

In every celebration for the dead, the Church attaches great importance to the reading of the word of God. The readings proclaim to the assembly the paschal mystery, teach remembrance of the dead, convey the hope of being gathered together again in God's kingdom, and encourage the witness of Christian life. Above all, the readings tell of God's designs for a world in which suffering and death will relinquish their hold on all whom God has called his own.

A careful selection and use of readings from Scripture for the funeral rites will provide the family and the community with an opportunity to hear God speak to them in their needs, sorrows, fears and hopes. The readings in this volume contain the readings proposed in the Order of Christian Funerals, with comments that may help in the choice of suitable Scripture passages. It can be used at home with the family in the selection of readings, in the choice of readers and their preparation.

These readings speak to all who are present at the funeral about the meaning of death, about the deceased person and about all who mourn. They recall us all to an understanding of death as part of our own lives. It is important that they be read well. Understandably, the reader may find that the emotions of the occasion add to the difficulty of public reading. It will help if he or she has had time to become familiar with the passage to be read. Many of the texts are familiar, but they will take on added meaning in the circumstances. They will be the basis of the preacher's homily, in which he will remind us of the mystery of God's compassionate love and the mystery of Jesus' victorious death and resurrection lived out in the one whom we mourn. This will be reinforced if the reading of the word of God has been done properly and prayerfully.

The biblical readings are the expression of our Christian faith in the paschal mystery and our hope in future resurrection. Sometimes the deceased may have expressed a desire for a favourite passage of Scripture which is not in the funeral rites selection. This will normally be acceptable. The use of other passages of literature is another matter. In the celebration of the liturgy of the word at the funeral liturgy, the biblical readings may not be replaced by non-biblical readings. But during prayer services with the family, non-biblical readings may be used in addition to readings from Scripture. These passages may also be useful as illustration when the deceased person's life is being spoken about. Such choices have to be made with sensitivity to the feelings of all at this time, but also with respect for the integrity of the liturgy being celebrated. In particular, we must avoid the extremes of, on the one hand, an excessive resurrectionist joy, out of touch with the state of the bereaved, and, on the other, a fear of affirming their faith and hope because of concern for their emotional state.

HOW TO PREPARE

The texts are generally quite short and straightforward. This is a help if you are nervous, but it does mean that you have to ensure that the message gets across to those who are listening.

First, make sure that you have no problems with pronunciation. Read the text out loud to get the feel of the sentences. Remember that you will tend to read too fast, so learn to pause and control your speech. Be clear about what the main point of the passage is. The sentence in italics is there to help you see the main point. It is not to be read out loud. Remember that the congregation will be particularly interested on this occasion in what is being said. They will not be so concerned with how you read as with what you are saying. You are sharing in the work of building up their faith and hope, helping to give comfort and consolation.

A word about the Responsorial Psalm. This may be sung, but if it is to be read, remember that it is a poem and has a musical rhythm. An introduction is supplied here for each psalm to help people to understand what the prayer is about. The reader should help the congregation to remember the response by repeating it with them, but should never cue them in by saying: 'Response!'

THE CHOICE OF READINGS

The following are suggested as suitable readings for particular persons. It is not an exhaustive list, and each reading in the Lectionary does express the message of Christian faith, hope and love.

1R = First Readings from the Old Testament
1RNT = First Readings from the New Testament used at Easter
2R = New Testament Readings
G = Gospel
The numbering is as in this book and in the Lectionary, Vol III.

In deep grief 1R, G15
Sinners 2R1, 2R2, G8
After suffering or deprivation 2R5, 2R9, G1, G19
One in service of others 2R6, 2R15, G4
An exile, or lonely person 2R10, G1
The handicapped 2R8, 2R9, 2R11
One noted for charity 1R3, 2R6, 2R15, G4,G9
One who has given his or her life 2R4,G16
A bishop or priest 1R6, 1RNT1, 2R5, 2R13, G10,G18
A deacon 1R6, 1RNT1, 2R13, 2R15, G4, G10,G18
Teachers 1R6
A religious 1RNT2, 2R5, 2R21, G4, G9, G14, G17, G18
A minister of the Eucharist G13
One who worked in the service of the Gospel 1RNT3, 2R5, 2R6, 2R13,
        G4, G9, G18
An unusual Christian G17
A husband or wife 1R4, 2R4
A parent 2R14, G4
An only child G6
One who died young 1R2, 1R3
One advanced in age 1R5, G4, G7
One who died after a long illness 1R2, 2R4, 2R9, G2, G7, G19
One who died suddenly G3, G7, G16
One who died by suicide 2R1, G8, G17
Several persons 1RNT2, 1RNT3, 2R6

The following texts are from the Jerusalem Bible.

Old Testament

READING I

*These are words of trust expressed when all seems hopeless. In Jewish law the
nearest relative was to stand in support of someone in grave need – this was*

the Avenger or Redeemer. We have faith in the concern of the redeeming Christ for each one of us as near and dear to him. He will restore our mortal bodies and we shall see God.

A reading from the book of Job 19:1.23-27

This I know: that my Avenger lives.

Job said:

'Ah, would that these words of mine were written down,
inscribed on some monument
with iron chisel and engraving tool,
cut into the rock for ever.
This I know: that my Avenger lives,
and he, the Last, will take his stand on earth.
After my awaking, he will set me close to him,
and from my flesh I shall look on God.
He whom I shall see will take my part:
these eyes will gaze on him and find him not aloof.'
This is the word of the Lord.

READING 2

We are asked to look on this death not from our angle but from God's. To us it is a tragedy and a grave loss. But God has tested and tried his loved one. Death is not the end but the refining process by which the faithful are made worthy to live with God in love.

A reading from the book of Wisdom 3:1-9

He accepted them as a holocaust.

The souls of the virtuous are in the hands of God,
no torment shall ever touch them.
In the eyes of the unwise, they did appear to die,
their going looked like a disaster,
their leaving us, like annihilation;
but they are in peace.
If they experienced punishment as men see it,
their hope was rich with immortality;

slight was their affliction, great will their blessings be.
God has put them to the test
and proved them worthy to be with him;
he has tested them like gold in a furnace,
and accepted them as a holocaust.
When the time comes for his visitation they will shine out;
as sparks run through the stubble, so will they.
They shall judge nations, rule over peoples,
and the Lord will be their king for ever.
They who trust in him will understand the truth,
those who are faithful will live with him in love;
for grace and mercy await those he has chosen.
      This is the word of the Lord.

READING 3

The number of years we live is not the measure of our greatness or holiness. This death does not seem to have any meaning to us, but who knows the mind of God? Ripeness is all, and in a short time this soul has come to perfection. This is one pleasing to God and preserved from further temptation to evil.

A reading from the book of Wisdom   4:7-15

Untarnished life, this is ripe old age.

The virtuous man, though he die before his time, will find rest.
Length of days is not what makes age honourable,
nor number of years the true measure of life;
understanding, this is man's grey hairs,
untarnished life, this is ripe old age.
He has sought to please God, so God has loved him;
as he was living among sinners, he has been taken up.
He has been carried off so that evil may not warp his understanding
or treachery seduce his soul;
for the fascination of evil throws good things into the shade,
and the whirlwind of desire corrupts a simple heart.
Coming to perfection in so short a while, he achieved long life;
his soul being pleasing to the Lord,
he has taken him quickly from the wickedness around him.

Yet people look on, uncomprehending;
it does not enter their heads
that grace and mercy await the chosen of the Lord,
and protection, his holy ones.
>   This is the word of the Lord.

READING 4

When we celebrate Mass and receive our Lord in Holy Communion we do so in joyful hope of taking part in the eternal banquet at the heavenly table. This reading reminds us that we will all be reunited at that table, and all mourning will be turned into joy.

A reading from the prophet Isaiah   25:6-9

The Lord will destroy Death for ever.

On this mountain,
the Lord of hosts will prepare for all peoples
a banquet of rich food.
On this mountain he will remove
the mourning veil covering all peoples,
and the shroud enwrapping all nations,
he will destroy Death for ever.
The Lord will wipe away
the tears from every cheek;
he will take away his people's shame
everywhere on earth,
for the Lord has said so.
That day, it will be said: See, this is our God
in whom we hoped for salvation;
the Lord is the one in whom we hoped.
We exult and we rejoice
that he has saved us.
>   This is the word of the Lord.

READING 5

This death has left us all shattered and bereft. How can we face the future without the one who is gone from our midst? In this reading the prophet has seen Jerusalem destroyed and he has to live without all that he has held dear. But he remembers God's love in the past and trusts him for the future. New every morning are God's many mercies to us.

A reading from the book of Lamentations   3:17-26

It is good to wait in silence for the Lord to save.

My soul is shut out from peace;
I have forgotten happiness.
And now I say, 'My strength is gone,
that hope which came from the Lord'.
Brooding on my anguish and affliction
is gall and wormwood.
My spirit ponders it continually
and sinks within me.
This is what I shall tell my heart,
and so recover hope:
the favours of the Lord are not all past,
his kindnesses are not exhausted;
every morning they are renewed;
great is his faithfulness.
'My portion is the Lord' says my soul
'and so I will hope in him.'
The Lord is good to those who trust him,
to the soul that searches for him.
It is good to wait in silence
for the Lord to save.
            This is the word of the Lord.

READING 6

We who have experienced the wise help and guidance of our friend who has died can rejoice at the words of comfort in this reading. There is great reward for all who have instructed many in virtue by teaching and example.

A reading from the prophet Daniel   *12:1-3*

Those who lie sleeping in the dust will awake.

I, Daniel, was doing penance when I received this message from the
Lord:
'At that time Michael will stand up, the great prince who mounts
guard over your people. There is going to be a time of great distress,
unparalleled since nations first came into existence. When that time
comes, your own people will be spared, all those whose names are
found written in the Book. Of those who lie sleeping in the dust of
the earth many will awake, some to everlasting life, some to shame
and everlasting disgrace. The learned will shine as brightly as the vault
of heaven, and those who have instructed many in virtue, as bright as
stars for all eternity.'
This is the word of the Lord.

READING 7

*The people of God were led slowly to an understanding of the next life. This
reading shows how prayer and sacrifice for the dead are seen as good and
profitable. We trust that our prayers at this Mass may release our friend from
all sin.*

A reading from the second book of Maccabees   *12:43-45*

A fine and noble action, in which he took account of the resurrection.

Judas, the leader of the Jews, took a collection from the people indi-
vidually, amounting to nearly two thousand drachmae, and sent it to
Jerusalem to have a sacrifice for sin offered, an altogether fine and
noble action, in which he took full account of the resurrection. For if
he had not expected the fallen to rise again it would have been super-
fluous and foolish to pray for the dead, whereas if he had in view the
splendid recompense reserved for those who make a pious end, the
thought was holy and devout. This was why he had this atonement
sacrifice offered for the dead, so that they might be released from their
sin.
This is the word of the Lord.

New Testament

First Reading from the New Testament

READING I

The first message of the Apostles is that faith in Jesus Christ leads to forgiveness of sins and gives us confidence when we appear before God, the judge of the living and the dead.

A reading from the Acts of the Apostles   *10:34-43*

God has appointed him to judge everyone, alive or dead.

Peter addressed Cornelius and his household:
'The truth I have now come to realise,' he said, 'is that God does not have favourites, but that anybody of any nationality who fears God and does what is right is acceptable to him.
'It is true, God sent his word to the people of Israel, and it was to them that the good news of peace was brought by Jesus Christ – but Jesus Christ is Lord of all men. 'You must have heard about the recent happenings in Judaea; about Jesus of Nazareth and how he began in Galilee, after John had been preaching baptism. God had anointed him with the Holy Spirit and with power, and because God was with him, Jesus went about doing good and curing all who had fallen into the power of the devil. Now I, and those with me, can witness to everything he did throughout the countryside of Judaea and in Jerusalem itself: and also to the fact that they killed him by hanging him on a tree, yet three days afterwards God raised him to life and allowed him to be seen, not by the whole people but only by certain witnesses God had chosen beforehand. Now we are those witnesses – we have eaten and drunk with him after his resurrection from the dead – and he has ordered us to proclaim this to his people and to tell them that God has appointed him to judge everyone alive or dead. It is to him that all the prophets bear this witness: that all who believe in Jesus will have their sins forgiven through his name.'
This is the word of the Lord.

READING 2

We, who mourn the death of one who was in every way such a faithful Christian, can take comfort from these words. This well-lived life merits a great reward.

A reading from the book of Revelation   *14:13*

Happy are those who die in the Lord!

I, John, heard a voice from heaven say to me, 'Write down: Happy are those who die in the Lord! Happy indeed, the Spirit says; now they can rest for ever after their work, since their good deeds go with them.'

This is the word of the Lord.

READING 3

The prophet reminds us that this world is passing away, and what is of importance is the good we do with our lives. The one permanent feature is the everlasting God. To be with him for ever is our hope.

A reading from the book of Revelation   *20:11-21:1*

The dead were judged according to what they had done in their lives.

I, John, saw a great white throne and the One who was sitting on it. In his presence, earth and sky vanished, leaving no trace. I saw the dead, both great and small, standing in front of his throne, while the book of life was opened, and other books opened which were the record of what they had done in their lives, by which the dead were judged.

The sea gave up all the dead who were in it; Death and Hades were emptied of the dead that were in them; and every one was judged according to the way in which he had lived. Then Death and Hades were thrown into the burning lake. This burning lake is the second death; and anybody whose name could not be found written in the book of life was thrown into the burning lake.

Then I saw a new heaven and a new earth; the first heaven and the first earth had disappeared now, and there was no longer any sea.

This is the word of the Lord.

READING 4

This reading gives us a picture of happiness in heaven where mourning and weeping are no more. We should not regret that our friend is now part of that eternal joy.

A reading from the book of Revelation   *21:1-7*

There will be no more death.

I, John, saw a new heaven and a new earth; the first heaven and the first earth had disappeared now, and there was no longer any sea. I saw the holy city, and the new Jerusalem, coming down from God out of heaven, as beautiful as a bride all dressed for her husband. Then I heard a loud voice call from the throne, 'You see this city? Here God lives among men. He will make his home among them; they shall be his people, and he will be their God; his name is God-with-them. He will wipe away all tears from their eyes; there will be no more death, and no more mourning or sadness. The world of the past has gone'.
Then the One sitting on the throne spoke: 'Now I am making the whole of creation new,' he said. 'I will give water from the well of life free to anybody who is thirsty; it is the rightful inheritance of the one who proves victorious; and I will be his God and he a son to me.'
This is the word of the Lord.

Second Reading from the New Testament

READING I

We can console ourselves that God showed his love for us in that while we were sinners Christ died for us. He is not going to abandon us now but supports us through life into death.

A reading from the letter of St Paul to the Romans   *5:5-11*

Having died to make us righteous, is it likely that he would now fail to save us from God's anger?

Hope is not deceptive, because the love of God has been poured into our hearts by the Holy Spirit which has been given us. We were still helpless when at his appointed moment Christ died for sinful men. It is not easy to die even for a good man – though of course for someone really worthy, a man might be prepared to die – but what proves that God loves us is that Christ died for us while we were still sinners. Having died to make us righteous, is it likely that he would now fail to save us from God's anger? When we were reconciled to God by the death of his Son, we were still enemies; now that we have been reconciled, surely we may count on being saved by the life of his Son? Not merely because we have been reconciled but because we are filled with joyful trust in God, through our Lord Jesus Christ, through whom we have already gained our reconciliation.

This is the word of the Lord.

READING 2

No matter how much sin there may be in our lives, the grace won for us by Christ overcomes it. Christ through his death on the cross in obedience to the Father has healed the consequences of our disobedience.

A reading from the letter of St Paul to the Romans *5:17-21*

However great the number of sins committed, grace was even greater.

If it is certain that death reigned over everyone as the consequence of one man's fall, it is even more certain that one man, Jesus Christ, will cause everyone to reign in life who receives the free gift that he does not deserve, of being made righteous. Again, as one man's fall brought condemnation on everyone, so the good act of one man brings everyone life and makes them justified. As by one man's disobedience many were made sinners, so by one man's obedience many will be made righteous. When law came, it was to multiply the opportunities of falling, but however great the number of sins committed, grace was even greater; and so, just as sin reigned wherever there was death, so grace will reign to bring eternal life thanks to the righteousness that comes through Jesus Christ our Lord.

This is the word of the Lord.

READING 3

Our friend who has died was once baptised into the life of Christ. That life comes to fulfilment now in a sharing in the fullness of Christ's resurrection.

A reading from the letter of St Paul to the Romans   *6:3-9*

Let us live a new life.

When we were baptised in Christ Jesus we were baptised in his death; in other words, when we were baptised we went into the tomb with him and joined him in death, so that as Christ was raised from the dead by the Father's glory, we too might live a new life.

If in union with Christ we have imitated his death, we shall also imitate him in his resurrection. We must realise that our former selves have been crucified with him to destroy this sinful body and to free us from the slavery of sin. When a man dies, of course, he has finished with sin.

But we believe that having died with Christ we shall return to life with him: Christ, as we know, having been raised from the dead will never die again. Death has no power over him any more.

This is the word of the Lord.

READING 4

Through Christ we are God's own children. We share in the life of Christ, and we share also in his sufferings. Long illness and much pain can bring us close to the passion of Christ, and enable us to share also in his resurrection and glorification.

A reading from the letter of St Paul to the Romans   *8:14-23*

We wait for our bodies to be set free.

Everyone moved by the Spirit is a son of God. The spirit you received is not the spirit of slaves bringing fear into your lives again; it is the spirit of sons, and it makes us cry out, 'Abba, Father!' The Spirit himself and our spirit bear united witness that we are children of God. And if we are children we are heirs as well: heirs of God and coheirs with Christ, sharing his sufferings so as to share his glory.

I think that what we suffer in this life can never be compared to the glory, as yet unrevealed, which is waiting for us. The whole creation is eagerly waiting for God to reveal his sons. It was not for any fault on the part of creation that it was made unable to attain its purpose, it was made so by God; but creation still retains the hope of being freed, like us, from its slavery to decadence, to enjoy the same freedom and glory as the children of God. From the beginning till now the entire creation, as we know, has been groaning in one great act of giving birth; and not only creation, but all of us who possess the first-fruits of the spirit, we too groan inwardly as we wait for our bodies to be set free.

    This is the word of the Lord.

READING 5

God's love for us is shown in the sufferings and death of Jesus Christ. He will never abandon us. We must trust in him despite all the things that may come against us in life. And death itself brings us into the fullness of God's love.

A reading from the letter of St Paul to the Romans   *8:31-35. 37-39*

Nothing can come between us and the love of Christ.

With God on our side who can be against us? Since God did not spare his own Son, but gave him up to benefit us all, we may be certain, after such a gift, that he will not refuse anything he can give. Could anyone accuse those that God has chosen? When God acquits, could anyone condemn? Could Christ Jesus? No! He not only died for us – he rose from the dead, and there at God's right hand he stands and pleads for us.

Nothing therefore can come between us and the love of Christ, even if we are troubled or worried, or being persecuted, or lacking food or clothes, or being threatened or even attacked. These are the trials through which we triumph, by the power of him who loved us.

For I am certain of this; neither death nor life, no angel, no prince, nothing that exists, nothing still to come, not any power, or height or depth, nor any created thing, can ever come between us and the love of God made visible in Christ Jesus our Lord.

    This is the word of the Lord.

READING 6

In life and in death we belong to God, for Christ is Lord of the living and the dead. But we do not live in isolation from other people; we have an influence on others for good or bad. Our friend's work for others will be well rewarded.

A reading from the letter of St Paul to the Romans   *14:7-12*

Alive or dead, we belong to the Lord.

The life and death of each of us has its influence on others; if we live, we live for the Lord; and if we die, we die for the Lord, so that alive or dead we belong to the Lord. This explains why Christ both died and came to life, it was so that he might be Lord both of the dead and of the living. We shall all have to stand before the judgement seat of God; as scripture says: By my life – it is the Lord who speaks – every knee shall bend before me, and every tongue shall praise God. It is to God, therefore, that each of us must give an account of himself.
        This is the word of the Lord.

READING 7

Each of us in our time comes to the moment of death. And as Christ overcame death so we through the power of his resurrection come to eternal life. In the kingdom of God the Father we shall all be reunited.

A reading from the first letter of St Paul to the Corinthians   *15:20-28*

All men will be brought to life in Christ.

Christ has been raised from the dead, the first-fruits of all who have fallen asleep. Death came through one man and in the same way the resurrection of the dead has come through one man. Just as all men die in Adam, so all men will be brought to life in Christ, but all of them in their proper order; Christ as the first-fruits and then, after the coming of Christ, those who belong to him. After that will come the end, when he hands over the kingdom to God the Father. For he must be king until he has put all his enemies under his feet and the last of the enemies to be destroyed is death, for everything is to be put under his feet. – Though when it is said that everything is subjected, this clearly cannot include the One who subjected everything to him. And when everything is subjected to him, then the Son himself will be subject in his turn to the One who subjected all things to him, so that God may be all in all.

This is the word of the Lord.

READING 8

Death is our entry into glory. Through death we gain the victory over the weakness of our human nature; we defeat death by no longer being subject to decay. We should always be thankful for the victory of Christ.

A reading from the first letter of St Paul to the Corinthians   *15:51-57*

Death is swallowed up in victory.

I will tell you something that has been secret: that we are not all going to die, but we shall all be changed. This will be instantaneous, in the twinkling of an eye, when the last trumpet sounds. It will sound, and the dead will be raised, imperishable, and we shall be changed as well, because our present perishable nature must put on imperishability, and this mortal nature must put on immortality.

When this perishable nature has put on imperishability, and when this mortal nature has put on immortality, then the words of scripture will come true: Death is swallowed up in victory. Death, where is your victory? Death, where is your sting? Now the sting of death is sin, and sin gets its power from the Law. So let us thank God for giving us the victory through our Lord Jesus Christ.

This is the word of the Lord.

READING 9

If we are really wise we will put our trust in permanent realities, not in the passing things of this world which perish before our eyes. Dealing well with the things of this life trains us to carry the glory that will be ours in the life to come.

A reading from the second letter of St Paul to the Corinthians *4:14-5:1*

Visible things last only for a time, but the invisible are eternal.

We know that he who raised the Lord Jesus to life will raise us with Jesus in our turn, and put us by his side and you with us. You see, all this is for your benefit, so that the more grace is multiplied among people, the more thanksgiving there will be, to the glory of God.

That is why there is no weakening on our part, and instead, though this outer man of ours may be falling into decay, the inner man is renewed day by day. Yes the troubles which are soon over, though they weigh little, train us for the carrying of a weight of eternal glory which is out of all proportion to them. And so we have no eyes for things that are visible, but only for things that are invisible; for visible things last only for a time, and the invisible things are eternal.

For we know that when the tent that we live in on earth is folded up, there is a house built by God for us, an everlasting home not made by human hands, in the heavens.

This is the word of the Lord.

READING 10

As we mourn the death of our loved friend, we feel the shortness of human life. How quickly it passes away! Our human life is only a temporary home, where we wait for our permanent dwelling in heaven.

A reading from the second letter of St Paul to the Corinthians *5:1. 6-10*

We have an everlasting home in the heavens.

We know that when the tent that we live in on earth is folded up, there is a house built by God for us, an everlasting home not made by human hands, in the heavens.

We are always full of confidence, then, when we remember that to live in the body means to be exiled from the Lord, going as we do by faith and not by sight – we are full of confidence, I say, and actually want to be exiled from the body and make our home with the Lord. Whether we are living in the body or exiled from it, we are intent on pleasing him. For all the truth about us will be brought out in the law court of Christ, and each of us will get what he deserves for the things he did in the body, good or bad.

This is the word of the Lord.

READING 11

Death is a return home. Since our baptism we really belong in God's kingdom. Death will complete the transformation begun then, and even our mortal bodies will share that transformation into perfect bodies.

A reading from the letter of St Paul to the Philippians　　　*3:20-21*

He will transfigure these wretched bodies of ours into copies of his glorious body.

For us, our homeland is in heaven, and from heaven comes the saviour we are waiting for, the Lord Jesus Christ, and he will transfigure these wretched bodies of ours into copies of his glorious body. He will do that by the same power with which he can subdue the whole universe.

This is the word of the Lord.

READING 12

The cross of Christ is the cause of our hope. And having hope we are not to mourn and grieve as if we hadn't. Rather we must comfort one another with the knowledge that our friend who has left us shares now the victory of Christ before us.

A reading from the first letter of St Paul to the Thessalonians　*4:13-18*

We shall stay with the Lord for ever.

We want you to be quite certain, brothers, about those who have died, to make sure that you do not grieve about them, like the other people who have no hope. We believe that Jesus died and rose again, and that it will be the same for those who have died in Jesus: God will bring them with him. We can tell you this from the Lord's own teaching, that any of us who are left alive until the Lord's coming will not have any advantage over those who have died. At the trumpet of God, the voice of the archangel will call out the command and the Lord himself will come down from heaven; those who have died in Christ will be the first to rise, and then those of us who are still alive will be taken up in the clouds, together with them, to meet the Lord in the air. So we shall stay with the Lord for ever. With such thoughts as these you should comfort one another.

This is the word of the Lord.

READING 13

Christian hope in the resurrection is unshakeable. St Paul, bound in prison, expresses that hope in this reading. One who has spent his life in Christ will rise with him.

A reading from the second letter of St Paul to Timothy   *2:8-13*

If we die with him, then we shall live with him.

Remember the Good News that I carry, 'Jesus Christ risen from the dead, sprung from the race of David'; it is on account of this that I have my own hardships to bear, even to being chained like a criminal – but they cannot chain up God's news. So I hear it all for the sake of those who are chosen so that in the end they may have the salvation that is in Christ Jesus and the eternal glory that comes with it.
Here is a saying that you can rely on:
If we have died with him, then we shall live with him.
If we hold firm, then we shall reign with him.
If we disown him, then he will disown us.
We may be unfaithful, but he is always faithful,
for he cannot disown his own self.

This is the word of the Lord.

READING 14

To be baptised as a Christian is already a great privilege and dignity. But the future life of heaven is beyond all our understanding, because it is a share in the very life of God himself. Through death we break through the veil and see into that marvellous existence.

A reading from the first letter of St John   *3:1-2*

We shall see him as he really is.

Think of the love that the Father has lavished on us,
by letting us be called God's children;
and that is what we are.
Because the world refused to acknowledge him,
therefore it does not acknowledge us.
My dear people, we are already the children of God
but what we are to be in the future has not yet been revealed;
all we know is, that when it is revealed
we shall be like him
because we shall see him as he really is.
       This is the word of the Lord.

READING 15

Love is life-giving. Our friend for whom we mourn gave an example of un-selfish love for others. St John says that such love conquers death and gives life. As Christ loved and now lives so do all who act from love.

A reading from the first letter of St John   *3:14-16*

We have passed out of death and into life because we love our brothers.

We have passed out of death and into life,
and of this we can be sure
because we love our brothers.
If you refuse to love, you must remain dead;
to hate your brother is to be a murderer,
and murderers, as you know, do not have eternal life in them.
This has taught us love –
that he gave up his life for us;
and we, too, ought to give up our lives for our brothers.
       This is the word of the Lord.

Gospels and Gospel Acclamations

READING I

The Beatitudes are an expression of the Christian way of life. They measure how much we resemble Christ. The one we mourn today tried to live by the standards they set. For such a life the reward is the kingdom of heaven.

Gospel Acclamation   *Mt 25:34*

Alleluia, alleluia!
Come, you whom my Father has blessed,
says the Lord;
take for your heritage the kingdom prepared for you
since the foundation of the world.
Alleluia!

A reading from the holy Gospel according to Matthew   *5:1-12*

Rejoice and be glad, for your reward will be great in heaven.

Seeing the crowds, Jesus went up the hill. There he sat down and was joined by his disciples. Then he began to speak. This is what he taught them:

'How happy are the poor in spirit:
theirs is the kingdom of heaven.
Happy the gentle:
they shall have the earth for their heritage.
Happy those who mourn:
they shall be comforted.
Happy those who hunger and thirst for what is right:
they shall be satisfied.
Happy the merciful:
they shall have mercy shown them.
Happy the pure in heart:
they shall see God.
Happy the peacemakers:

they shall be called sons of God.
Happy those who are persecuted in the cause of right:
theirs is the kingdom of heaven.

'Happy are you when people abuse you and persecute you and speak
all kinds of calumny against you on my account. Rejoice and be glad,
for your reward will be great in heaven.'
This is the Gospel of the Lord.

READING 2

*The thought of death and the shortness of life can teach us true wisdom. The
gentleness and humility of Christ urge us to keep our lives in proper perspec-
tive. Eternal rest is the reward of those who follow Christ's way.*

Gospel Acclamation   *cf. Mt 11:25*

Alleluia, alleluia!
Blessed are you, Father,
Lord of heaven and earth;
for revealing the mysteries of the Kingdom
to mere children.
Alleluia!

A reading from the holy Gospel according to Matthew   *11:25-30*

Come to me, and I will give you rest.

Jesus exclaimed, 'I bless you, Father, Lord of heaven and of earth, for
hiding these things from the learned and the clever and revealing
them to mere children. Yes, Father, for that is what it pleased you to
do. Everything has been entrusted to me by my Father; and no one
knows the Son except the Father, just as no one knows the Father except the Son and those to whom the Son chooses to reveal him.
'Come to me, all you who labour and are overburdened, and I will
give you rest. Shoulder my yoke and learn from me, for I am gentle
and humble in heart, and you will find rest for your souls. Yes, my
yoke is easy and my burden light.'
This is the Gospel of the Lord.

READING 3

Death is the most important moment of our lives. We do not know when it will come, but we have to be ready. The one we mourn was always watchful and waiting, and ready with the light of baptism still burning brightly.

Gospel Acclamation

cf. Phil 3:20

Alleluia, alleluia!
Our homeland is in heaven,
and from heaven comes the Saviour we are waiting for,
the Lord Jesus Christ.
Alleluia!

A reading from the holy Gospel according to Matthew

25:1-13

The bridegroom is here! Go out and meet him.

Jesus spoke this parable to his disciples: 'The kingdom of heaven will be like this: Ten bridesmaids took their lamps and went to meet the bridegroom. Five of them were foolish and five were sensible: the foolish ones did take their lamps, but they brought no oil, whereas the sensible ones took flasks of oil as well as their lamps. The bridegroom was late and they all grew drowsy and fell asleep. But at midnight there was a cry. "The bridegroom is here! Go out and meet him." At this, all those bridesmaids woke up and trimmed their lamps, and the foolish ones said to the sensible ones, "Give us some of your oil: our lamps are going out". But they replied, "There may not be enough for us and for you; you had better go to those who sell it and buy some for yourselves". They had gone off to buy it when the bridegroom arrived. Those who were ready went in with him to the wedding hall and the door was closed. The other bridesmaids arrived later. "Lord, Lord," they said, "open the door for us." But he replied, "I tell you solemnly, I do not know you". So stay awake, because you do not know either the day or the hour'.
    This is the Gospel of the Lord.

READING 4

How do we judge the value of a well-spent life? This gospel parable tells us how God will judge us as Christians. Have we seen Christ in all the needy?

Gospel Acclamation   *Mt 25:34*

Alleluia, alleluia!
Come, you whom my Father has blessed,
says the Lord;
take for your heritage the kingdom prepared for you
since the foundation of the world.
Alleluia!

A reading from the holy Gospel according to Matthew   *25:31-46*

Come, you whom my Father has blessed.

Jesus said to his disciples: 'When the Son of Man comes in his glory, escorted by all the angels, then he will take his seat on his throne of glory. All the nations will be assembled before him and he will separate men one from another as the shepherd separates sheep from goats. He will place the sheep on his right hand and the goats on his left. Then the King will say to those on his right hand, "Come, you whom my Father has blessed, take for your heritage the kingdom prepared for you since the foundation of the world. For I was hungry and you gave me food; I was thirsty and you gave me drink; I was a stranger and you made me welcome; naked and you clothed me, sick and you visited me, in prison and you came to see me." Then the virtuous will say to him in reply, "Lord, when did we see you hungry and feed you; or thirsty and give you drink? When did we see you a stranger and make you welcome; naked and clothe you; sick or in prison and go to see you?" And the King will answer, "I tell you solemnly, in so far as you did this to one of the least of these brothers of mine, you did it to me." Next he will say to those on his left hand, "Go away from me, with your curse upon you, to the eternal fire prepared for the devil and his angels. For I was hungry and you never gave me food; I was thirsty and you never gave me anything to drink; I was a stranger and you never made me welcome, naked and you never clothed me, sick and in prison and you never visited me." Then it will be their turn to ask, "Lord, when did we see you hungry or thirsty, a stranger or naked, sick or in prison, and did not come to your help?" Then he will answer, "I tell you solemnly, in so far as you neglected to do this to one of the least of these, you neglected to do it to me." And they will go away to eternal punishment, and the virtuous to eternal life.'

    This is the Gospel of the Lord.

READING 5

The death of Jesus on the cross was a truly agonising experience. The onlookers shared the emotions of that occasion. Christ has shared with us the whole experience of death; but he has also given us the hope of resurrection.

Gospel Acclamation   *2 Tim 2:11-12*

Alleluia, alleluia!
If we have died with Christ, then we shall live with him.
If we hold firm, then
we shall reign with him.
Alleluia!

A reading from the holy Gospel according to Mark   *15:33-39; 16:1-6*

Jesus gave a loud cry and breathed his last.

When the sixth hour came there was darkness over the whole land until the ninth hour. And at the ninth hour Jesus cried out in a loud voice, 'Eloi, Eloi, lama sabachthani?' which means, 'My God, my God, why have you deserted me?' When some of those who stood by heard this, they said, 'Listen, he is calling on Elijah.' Someone ran and soaked a sponge in vinegar and, putting it on a reed, gave it him to drink saying, 'Wait and see if Elijah will come to take him down.' But Jesus gave a loud cry and breathed his last. And the veil of the Temple was torn in two from top to bottom. The centurion, who was standing in front of him, had seen how he had died and he said, 'In truth this man was a son of God.'

When the sabbath was over, Mary of Magdala, Mary the mother of James, and Salome, bought spices with which to go and anoint him. And very early in the morning on the first day of the week they went to the tomb, just as the sun was rising.

They had been saying to one another, 'Who will roll away the stone for us from the entrance to the tomb?' But when they looked they could see that the stone – which was very big – had already been rolled back. On entering the tomb they saw a young man in a white robe seated on the right-hand side, and they were struck with amazement. But he said to them, 'There is no need for alarm. You are looking for Jesus of Nazareth, who was crucified: he has risen, he is not here. See, here is the place where they laid him.'

This is the Gospel of the Lord.

READING 6

This gospel story shows us how God himself has compassion for us. It also shows the power of God who gives life. We know that he shares our grief this day. We rejoice also that he gives eternal life to the one we mourn.

Gospel Acclamation   *Jn 11:25-26*

Alleluia, alleluia!
I am the resurrection and the life,
says the Lord:
whoever believes in me will never die.
Alleluia!

A reading from the holy Gospel according to Luke   *7:11-17*

Young man, I tell you to get up.

Jesus went to a town call Nain, accompanied by his disciples and a great number of people. When he was near the gate of the town it happened that a dead man was being carried out for burial, the only son of his mother, and she was a widow. And a considerable number of the townspeople were with her. When the Lord saw her he felt sorry for her. 'Do not cry', he said. Then he went up and put his hand on the bier and the bearers stood still, and he said, 'Young man, I tell you to get up.' And the dead man sat up and began to talk, and Jesus gave him to his mother. Everyone was filled with awe and praised God saying, 'A great prophet has appeared among us; God has visited his people'. And this opinion of him spread throughout Judaea and all over the countryside.

This is the Gospel of the Lord.

READING 7

There are two pictures in this gospel passage: the anguish experienced by those who were not ready and watching when the thief came in the night, and the joy of those who, being ready, have the Master himself sharing their banquet.

Gospel Acclamation   *Phil 3:20*

Alleluia, alleluia!
Our homeland is in heaven,
and from heaven comes the Saviour we are waiting for,
the Lord Jesus Christ.
Alleluia!

A reading from the holy Gospel according to Luke   *12:35-40*

Stand ready.

Jesus said to his disciples: 'See that you are dressed for action and have your lamps lit. Be like men waiting for their master to return from the wedding feast, ready to open the door as soon as he comes and knocks. Happy those servants whom the master finds awake when he comes. I tell you solemnly, he will put on an apron, sit them down at table and wait on them. It may be in the second watch he comes, or in the third, but happy those servants if he finds them ready. You may be quite sure of this, that if the householder had known at what hour the burglar would come, he would not have let anyone break through the wall of the house. You too must stand ready, because the Son of Man is coming at an hour you do not expect.'
    This is the Gospel of the Lord.

READING 8

The repentant thief has given hope to many who at the last moment turned back to God. For our friend today and for all the departed we pray the words: Lord, remember me.

Gospel Acclamation   *Rv 14:13*

Alleluia, alleluia!
Happy are those who die in the Lord!
Now they can rest for ever after their work,
since their good deeds go with them.
Alleluia!

A reading from the holy Gospel according to Luke   *23:33. 39-43*

Today you will be with me in paradise.

When the soldiers reached the place called The Skull, they crucified
Jesus there and the two criminals also, one on the right, the other on
the left.
One of the criminals hanging there abused him. 'Are you not the
Christ?' he said. 'Save yourself and us as well.' But the other spoke up
and rebuked him. 'Have you no fear of God at all?' he said. 'You got
the same sentence as he did, but in our case we deserved it: we are
paying for what we did. But this man has done nothing wrong.
'Jesus,' he said, 'remember me when you come into your kingdom.'
'Indeed, I promise you,' he replied 'today you will be with me in paradise.'
        This is the Gospel of the Lord.

READING 9

*Jesus himself, facing the terror of death, could only commit himself in total
faith and trust to his Father. We commend our friend this day to the loving
care of our Father in heaven.*

Gospel Acclamation   *Rv 1:5-6*

Alleluia, alleluia!
Jesus Christ is the First-born from the dead;
to him be glory and power for ever and ever. Amen.
Alleluia!

A reading from the holy Gospel according to Luke

23:44-46. 50. 52-53. 24:1-6

Father, into your hands I commit my spirit.

It was about the sixth hour and, with the sun eclipsed, a darkness came over the whole land until the ninth hour. The veil of the Temple was torn right down the middle; and when Jesus had cried out in a loud voice, he said, 'Father, into your hands I commit my spirit'. With these words he breathed his last.

Then a member of the council arrived, an upright and virtuous man named Joseph. This man went to Pilate and asked for the body of Jesus. He then took it down, wrapped it in a shroud and put him in a tomb which was hewn in stone in which no one had yet been laid.

On the first day of the week, at the first sign of dawn, the women went to the tomb with the spices they had prepared. They found that the stone had been rolled away from the tomb, but on entering discovered that the body of the Lord Jesus was not there. As they stood there not knowing what to think, two men in brilliant clothes suddenly appeared at their side. Terrified, the women lowered their eyes. But the two men said to them, 'Why look among the dead for someone who is alive? He is not here; he has risen.'

This is the Gospel of the Lord.

READING 10

The risen body of Christ is so glorified that the disciples do not immediately recognise him. We too will rise with transformed bodies. As we approach the evening of life we pray for a deepening sense of his abiding presence with us.

Gospel Acclamation   *Jn 3:16*

Alleluia, alleluia!
God loved the world so much
that he gave his only Son;
everyone who believes in him has eternal life.
Alleluia!

A reading from the holy Gospel according to Luke   24:13-35

Was it not ordained that the Christ should suffer and enter into his glory?

On the first day of the week, two of the disciples were on their way to a village called Emmaus, seven miles from Jerusalem, and they were talking together about all that had happened. Now as they talked this over, Jesus himself came up and walked by their side; but something prevented them from recognising him. He said to them, 'What matters are you discussing as you walk along?' They stopped short, their faces downcast.

Then one of them, called Cleopas, answered him. 'You must be the only person staying in Jerusalem who does not know the things that have been happening there these last few days.' 'What things?' he asked. 'All about Jesus of Nazareth,' they answered, 'who proved he was a great prophet by the things he said and did in the sight of God and of the whole people; and how our chief priests and our leaders handed him over to be sentenced to death, and had him crucified. Our own hope had been that he would be the one to set Israel free. And this is not all: two whole days have gone by since it all happened; and some women from our group have astounded us; they went to the tomb in the early morning, and when they did not find the body, they came back to tell us they had seen a vision of angels who declared he was alive. Some of our friends went to the tomb and found everything exactly as the women had reported, but of him they saw nothing.'

Then he said to them, 'You foolish men! So slow to believe the full message of the prophets! Was it not ordained that the Christ should suffer and so enter into his glory?' Then, starting with Moses and going through all the prophets, he explained to them the passages throughout the scriptures that were about himself.

When they drew near to the village to which they were going, he made as if to go on; but they pressed him to stay with them. 'It is nearly evening,' they said, 'and the day is almost over.' So he went in to stay with them. Now while he was with them at table, he took the bread and said the blessing; then he broke it and handed it to them. And their eyes were opened and they recognised him; but he had vanished from their sight. Then they said to each other, 'Did not our hearts burn within us as he talked to us on the road and explained the scriptures to us?'

They set out that instant and returned to Jerusalem. There they found the Eleven assembled together with their companions, who said to

them, 'Yes, it is true. The Lord has risen and has appeared to Simon.'
Then they told their story of what had happened on the road and
how they had recognised him at the breaking of bread.

> This is the Gospel of the Lord.

READING 10

Shorter Form

A reading from the holy Gospel according to Luke   *24:13-16. 28-35*

Was it not ordained that the Christ should suffer and so enter into his glory?

On the first day of the week, two of the disciples were on their way to
a village called Emmaus, seven miles from Jerusalem, and they were
talking together about all that had happened. Now as they talked this
over, Jesus himself came up and walked by their side; but something
prevented them from recognising him.

When they drew near to the village to which they were going, he
made as if to go on; but they pressed him to stay with them. 'It is
nearly evening,' they said, 'and the day is almost over.' So he went in
to stay with them. Now while he was with them at table, he took the
bread and said the blessing; then he broke it and handed it to them.
And their eyes were opened and they recognised him; but he had vanished from their sight. Then they said to each other, 'Did not our
hearts burn within us as he talked to us on the road and explained the
scriptures to us?'

They set out that instant and returned to Jerusalem. There they found
the Eleven assembled together with their companions, who said to
them, 'Yes, it is true. The Lord has risen and has appeared to Simon.'
Then they told their story of what had happened on the road and
how they had recognised him at the breaking of bread.

> This is the Gospel of the Lord.

READING 11

*The path to a good Christian life is in listening to the word of God and obey-
ing it. One who has so lived need not fear death.*

Gospel Acclamation   *Mt 25:34*

Alleluia, alleluia!
Come, you whom my Father has blessed,
says the Lord;
take for your heritage the kingdom prepared for you
since the foundation of the world.
Alleluia!

A reading from the holy Gospel according to John   *5:24-29*

Whoever listens to my words and believes has passed from death to life.

Jesus said to the Jews:
    'I tell you most solemnly,
    whoever listens to my words,
    and believes in the one who sent me,
    has eternal life;
    without being brought to judgement
    he has passed from death to life.
    I tell you most solemnly,
    the hour will come – in fact it is here already –
    when the dead will hear the voice of the Son of God,
    and all who hear it will live.
    For the Father, who is the source of life,
    has made the Son the source of life;
    and, because he is the Son of Man,
    has appointed him supreme judge.
    Do not be surprised at this,
    for the hour is coming
    when the dead will leave their graves
    at the sound of his voice;
    those who did good
    will rise again to life;
    and those who did evil, to condemnation.
    I can do nothing by myself;
    I can only judge as I am told to judge,
    and my judging is just,
    because my aim is to do not my own will,
    but the will of him who sent me.'
        This is the Gospel of the Lord.

READING 12

Jesus Christ cares for us, because it is his Father's will that he should not lose us. We can only be lost through our own lack of faith and obedience.

Gospel Acclamation   *Jn 6:39*

Alleluia, alleluia!
It is my Father's will, says the Lord,
that I should lose nothing
of all that he has given to me,
and that I should raise it up on the last day.
Alleluia!

A reading from the holy Gospel according to John   *6:37-40*

Whoever believes in the Son has eternal life, and I shall raise him up on the last day.

Jesus said to the crowd:
  'All that the Father gives me will come to me,
  and whoever comes to me
  I shall not turn him away;
  because I have come from heaven,
  not to do my own will,
  but to do the will of the one who sent me.
  Now the will of him who sent me
  is that I should lose nothing
  of all that he has given to me,
  and that I should raise it up on the last day.
  Yes, it is my Father's will
  that whoever sees the Son and believes in him
  shall have eternal life,
  and that I shall raise him up on the last day.'
    This is the Gospel of the Lord.

READING 13

The mystery of faith we proclaim each day in the Mass is our union with Christ in his death and rising. Receiving the risen Lord in holy communion is our pledge of sharing in that risen life.

Gospel Acclamation   *Jn 6:51-52*

> Alleluia, alleluia!
> I am the living bread
> which has come down from heaven,
> says the Lord.
> Anyone who eats this bread
> will live for ever.
> Alleluia!

A reading from the holy Gospel according to John   *6:51-58*

Anyone who eats this bread has eternal life, and I shall raise him up on the last day.

> Jesus said to the crowd:
>> 'I am the living bread which has come down from heaven.
>> Anyone who eats this bread will live for ever;
>> and the bread that I shall give
>> is my flesh, for the life of the world.'
>> Then the Jews started arguing with one another: 'How can this man give us his flesh to eat?' they said. Jesus replied:
>> 'I tell you most solemnly,
>> if you do not eat the flesh of the Son of Man
>> and drink his blood,
>> you will not have life in you.
>> Anyone who does eat my flesh and drink my blood
>> has eternal life,
>> and I shall raise him up on the last day.
>> For my flesh is real food
>> and my blood is real drink.
>> He who eats my flesh and drinks my blood
>> lives in me,
>> and I live in him.

As I, who am sent by the living Father,
myself draw life from the Father,
so whoever eats me will draw life from me.
This is the bread come down from heaven;
not like the bread our ancestors ate:
they are dead,
but anyone who eats this bread will live for ever.'
      This is the Gospel of the Lord.

READING 14

We who need consolation today can share with all others who have treasured Jesus' words to Martha: 'I am the resurrection and the life.' Like her we must respond: 'I believe'.

Gospel Acclamation   *Jn 11:25.26*

Alleluia, alleluia!
I am the resurrection and the life,
says the Lord,
whoever believes in me will never die.
Alleluia!

A reading from the holy Gospel according to John   *11:17-21*

I am the resurrection and the life.

On arriving at Bethany, Jesus found that Lazarus had been in the tomb for four days already. Bethany is only about two miles from Jerusalem, and many Jews had come to Martha and Mary to sympathise with them over their brother. When Martha heard that Jesus had come she went to meet him. Mary remained sitting in the house. Martha said to Jesus, 'If you had been here, my brother would not have died, but I know that, even now, whatever you ask of God, he will grant you'. 'Your brother,' said Jesus to her, 'will rise again.' Martha said, 'I know he will rise again at the resurrection on the last day'. Jesus said:
      'I am the resurrection and the life.
      If anyone believes in me, even though he dies he will live,
      and whoever lives and believes in me
      will never die.

Do you believe this?'
'Yes, Lord,' she said, 'I believe that you are the Christ, the Son of
God, the one who was to come into this world.'
This is the Gospel of the Lord.

READING 15

*Christ shows that he gives life to the dead through this miracle of raising
Lazarus. It is a miracle worked so that we might have faith.*

Gospel Acclamation   *Jn 3:16*

Alleluia, alleluia!
God loved the world so much
that he gave his only Son;
everyone who believes in him has eternal life.
Alleluia!

A reading from the holy Gospel according to John   *11:32-45*

Lazarus, come out.

Mary the sister of Lazarus went to Jesus, and as soon as she saw him
she threw herself at his feet, saying, 'Lord, if you had been here, my
brother would not have died.' At the sight of her tears, and those of
the Jews who followed her, Jesus said in great distress, with a sigh that
came straight from the heart, 'Where have you put him?' They said,
'Lord, come and see'. Jesus wept; and the Jews said, 'See how much he
loved him!' But there were some who remarked, 'He opened the eyes
of the blind man, could he not have prevented this man's death?' Still
sighing, Jesus reached the tomb: it was a cave with a stone to close the
opening. Jesus said, 'Take the stone away.' Martha said to him, 'Lord,
by now he will smell; this is the fourth day.' Jesus replied, 'Have I not
told you that if you believe you will see the glory of God?' So they
took away the stone. Then Jesus lifted up his eyes and said:
'Father, I thank you for hearing my prayer.
I know indeed that you always hear me,
but I speak
for the sake of all these who stand round me,
so that they may believe it was you who sent me.'

When he had said this, he cried in a loud voice, 'Lazarus, here! Come out!' The dead man came out, his feet and hands bound with bands of stuff and a cloth round his face. Jesus said to them, 'Unbind him, let him go free.'
Many of the Jews who had come to visit Mary and had seen what he did believed in him.
      This is the Gospel of the Lord.

READING 16

The seed that is buried and rots in the ground might seem to be wasted, but it brings forth fruit in time. The life of the one we mourn today may seem to have achieved little or even to have been pointless. But God measures the giving and crowns the life with honour.

Gospel Acclamation   *Rv 14:13*

Alleluia, alleluia!
Happy are those who die in the Lord!
Now they can rest for ever after their work,
since their good deeds go with them.
Alleluia!

A reading from the holy Gospel according to John   *12:23-28*

If a wheat grain dies, it yields a rich harvest.

Jesus said to his disciples:
      'Now the hour has come
      for the Son of Man to be glorified.
      I tell you, most solemnly,
      unless a wheat grain falls on the ground and dies,
      it remains only a single grain;
      but if it dies,
      it yields a rich harvest.
      Anyone who loves his life loses it;
      anyone who hates his life in this world
      will keep it for the eternal life.
      If a man serves me, he must follow me,

wherever I am, my servant will be there too.
If anyone serves me, my Father will honour him.
Now my soul is troubled.
What shall I say:
Father, save me from this hour?
But it is for this very reason that I have come to this hour.
Father, glorify your name!'
A voice came from heaven, 'I have glorified it, and I will glorify it again.'

This is the Gospel of the Lord.

READING 17

God's judgements are not ours. We may not understand or appreciate the way of life of another, but the gospel reminds us that there are many ways to God, and many mansions in the kingdom.

Gospel Acclamation   *Jn 6:40*

Alleluia, alleluia!
It is my Father's will, says the Lord,
that whoever believes in the Son
shall have eternal life,
and that I shall raise him up on the last day.
Alleluia!

A reading from the holy Gospel according to John   *14:1-6*

There are many rooms in my Father's house.

Jesus said to his disciples:
    'Do not let your hearts be troubled.
    Trust in God still, and trust in me.
    There are many rooms in my Father's house;
    if there were not, I should have told you.
    I am going now to prepare a place for you,
    and after I have gone and prepared you a place,
    I shall return to take you with me;
    so that where I am

you may be too.
You know the way to the place where I am going.'
Thomas said, 'Lord, we do not know where you are going, so
how can we know the way?' Jesus said:
'I am the Way, the Truth and the Life.
No one can come to the Father except through me.'
This is the Gospel of the Lord.

READING 18

Jesus expressed his last wish for his followers, that they may follow his path to the Father. We can have hope and confidence today for the one we mourn since Christ wants him to be with him in paradise.

Gospel Acclamation   *Jn 6:39*

Alleluia, alleluia!
It is my Father's will, says the Lord,
that I shall lose nothing
of all that he has given to me,
and that I should raise it up on the last day.
Alleluia!

A reading from the holy Gospel according to John   *17:24-26*

I want them to be with me where I am.

Jesus raised his eyes to heaven and said:
'Father,
I want those you have given me
to be with me where I am,
so that they may always see the glory
you have given me
because you loved me
before the foundation of the world.
Father, Righteous One,
the world has not known you,
but I have known you,
and these have known
that you have sent me.

I have made your name known to them
and will continue to make it known
so that the love with which you loved me may be in them,
and so that I may be in them'.
    This is the Gospel of the Lord.

READING 19

Jesus was obedient to the Father even to the end. He gave up his life freely to him. We try to accept God's will in the midst of our suffering. That way leads to new life with the risen Christ. Joseph and Nicodemus remind us of the ministry of support to all who grieve.

Gospel Acclamation   *Jn 11:25.26*

Alleluia, alleluia!
I am the resurrection and the life,
says the Lord,
whoever believes in me will never die.
Alleluia!

A reading from the holy Gospel according to John   *19:17-18. 25-30*

Bowing his head he gave up his spirit.

Carrying his own cross, Jesus went out of the city to the place of the skull or, as it was called in Hebrew, Golgotha, where they crucified him with two others, one on either side with Jesus in the middle.
Near the cross of Jesus stood his mother and his mother's sister, Mary the wife of Clopas, and Mary of Magdala. Seeing his mother and the disciple he loved standing near her, Jesus said to his mother, 'Woman, this is your son'. Then to the disciple he said, 'This is your mother'.
After this, Jesus knew that everything had now been completed, and to fulfil the scripture perfectly he said:
    'I am thirsty'.
A jar full of vinegar stood there, so putting a sponge soaked in the vinegar on a hyssop stick they held it up to his mouth. After Jesus had taken the vinegar he said, 'It is accomplished'; and bowing his head he gave up his spirit.

It was Preparation Day, and to prevent the bodies remaining on the cross during sabbath – since that sabbath was a day of special solemnity – the Jews asked Pilate to have the legs broken and the bodies taken away. Consequently the soldiers came and broke the legs of the first man who had been crucified with him and then of the other. When they came to Jesus, they found he was already dead, and so instead of breaking his legs one of the soldiers pierced his side with a lance; and immediately there came out blood and water. This is the evidence of one who saw it – trustworthy evidence, and he knows he speaks the truth – and he gives it so that you may believe as well. Because all this happened to fulfil the words of scripture:

Not one bone of his will be broken;

and again, in another place scripture says:

They will look on the one whom they have pierced.

After this, Joseph of Arimathaea, who was a disciple of Jesus – though a secret one because he was afraid of the Jews – asked Pilate to let him remove the body of Jesus. Pilate gave permission, so they came and took it away. Nicodemus came as well – the same one who had first come to Jesus at night-time – and he brought a mixture of myrrh and aloes, weighing about a hundred pounds.

This is the Gospel of the Lord.

FOR THE BURIAL OF CHILDREN

I Burial of Baptised Children

Old Testament

READING 1

The prophet puts before us the vision of heaven where we shall all be reunited and where all weeping has ceased. This child has gone before us to the kingdom of God and we shall all meet again in joy.

A reading from the prophet Isaiah   *25:6. 7-9 Page 59*

The Lord will destroy Death for ever.

READING 2

The life of this child, short though it was, has been a blessing for us. And while we grieve over our loss, we can trust that the Lord never ceases to send us blessings for our consolation.

A reading from the book of Lamentations   *3:22-26*

It is good to wait in silence for the Lord to save.

> The favours of the Lord are not all past,
> his kindnesses are not exhausted;
> every morning they are renewed;
> great is his faithfulness.
> 'My portion is the Lord' says my soul
> 'and so I will hope in him.'
> The Lord is good to those who trust him,
> to the soul that searches for him.
> It is good to wait in silence
> for the Lord to save.
>   This is the word of the Lord.

First Reading from the New Testament

Baptised Children

READING I

All who now enjoy the presence of God in heaven are preserved from the tri-
als of life; they are at rest. We too, when our time of weeping is over, will
share in that joy.

A reading from the book of Revelation   7:9-10. 15-17

God will wipe away all tears from their eyes.

I, John, saw a huge number, impossible to count, of people from
every nation, race, tribe and language; they were standing in front of
the throne and in front of the Lamb, dressed in white robes and hold-
ing palms in their hands. They shouted aloud, 'Victory to our God,
who sits on the throne, and to the Lamb!' They now stand in front of
God's throne and serve him day and night in his sanctuary; and the
One who sits on the throne will spread his tent over them. They will
never hunger or thirst again; neither the sun nor scorching wind will
ever plague them, because the Lamb who is at the throne will be their
shepherd and will lead them to springs of living water; and God will
wipe away all tears from their eyes.
     This is the word of the Lord.

READING 2

Death brings a great sense of loss. This reading reminds us that it is tempo-
rary. Our days of pain and sorrow will end and God will heal all wounds.

A reading from the book of Revelation   21:1. 3-5

There will be no more death.

I, John, saw a new heaven and a new earth. Then I heard a loud voice call from the throne, 'You see this city? Here God lives among men. He will make his home among them; they shall be his people, and he will be their God; his name is God-with-them. He will wipe away all tears from their eyes; there will be no more death, and no more mourning or sadness. The world of the past has gone.'

Then the One sitting on the throne spoke: 'Now I am making the whole of creation new'.

This is the word of the Lord.

Second Reading from the New Testament

Baptised Children

READING 1

Our great consolation today is that this child received the life of Christ in baptism, and so now lives the new life with Christ in his kingdom.

A reading from the letter of St Paul to the Romans   *6:3-4. 8-9*

We believe that we shall return to life with Christ.

You have been taught that when we were baptised in Christ Jesus we were baptised in his death; in other words, when we were baptised we went into the tomb with him and joined him in death, so that as Christ was raised from the dead by the Father's glory, we too might live a new life.

We believe that having died with Christ we shall return to life with him: Christ, as we know, having been raised from the dead will never die again. Death has no power over him any more.

This is the word of the Lord.

READING 2

This child was given the precious gift of life, was reborn with new life in baptism, and now through the mystery of God's will has the fullness of life with him.

A reading from the letter of St Paul to the Romans   *14:7-9*

Alive or dead, we belong to the Lord.

The life and death of each of us has its influence on others; if we live, we live for the Lord; and if we die, we die for the Lord, so that alive or dead we belong to the Lord. This explains why Christ both died and came to life, it was so that he might be Lord both of the dead and of the living.
This is the word of the Lord.

READING 3

As human beings we are all subject to death, and we do not know when it will come to us. This child has been called sooner than us, and while we suffer in our loss, we know that it is a call to be happy with Christ.

A reading from the first letter of St Paul to the Corinthians   *15:20-23*

All men will be brought to life in Christ.

Christ has been raised from the dead, the first-fruits of all who have fallen asleep. Death came through one man and in the same way the resurrection of the dead has come through one man. Just as all men die in Adam, so all men will be brought to life in Christ; but all of them in their proper order; Christ as the first-fruits and then, after the coming of Christ, those who belong to him.
This is the word of the Lord.

READING 4

This reading thanks God for his choice of us. It is difficult to understand today why God chooses some sooner than others, but we recognise that choice as a favour.

A reading from the letter of St Paul to the Ephesians   *1:3-5*

Before the world was made God chose us in Christ.

Blessed be God the Father of our Lord Jesus Christ,
who has blessed us with all the spiritual blessings of heaven in Christ.
Before the world was made, he chose us, chose us in Christ,
to be holy and spotless, and to live through love in his presence,
determining that we should become his adopted sons, through Jesus
  Christ
for his own kind purposes.
   This is the word of the Lord.

READING 5

*Our grieving today is not that of those without hope. The pain of loss does
not blind us to the trust we have in God who now cares for our child.*

A reading from the first letter of St Paul to the Thessalonians   *4:13-14. 18*

We shall stay with the Lord for ever.

We want you to be quite certain, brothers, about those who have
died, to make sure that you do not grieve about them, like the other
people who have no hope. We believe that Jesus died and rose again,
and that it will be the same for those who have died in Jesus: God will
bring them with him. With such thoughts as these you should comfort one another.
   This is the word of the Lord.

Gospels and Gospel Acclamations

Baptised Children

READING 1

The vision of God that we all would like to attain is already given to this child – given by God's gracious will. Christ calls us to place our burden of sorrow on him that we may have relief.

Gospel Acclamation
cf. Mt 11:25

Alleluia, alleluia!
Blessed are you, Father,
Lord of heaven and of earth,
for revealing the mysteries of the kingdom
to children.
Alleluia!

A reading from the holy Gospel according to Matthew   11:25-30
Page 75

You have hidden these things from the clever, and have revealed them to mere children.

READING 2

Jesus told his disciples not to stop the little children coming to him. In our sorrow we are asked to bow to the will of God who has a special welcome for this child.

Gospel Acclamation
cf Mt 11:25

Alleluia, alleluia!
Blessed are you, Father,
Lord of heaven and of earth,
for revealing the mysteries of the kingdom
to children.
Alleluia!

A reading from the holy Gospel according to Mark   *10:13-16*

People were bringing little children to Jesus, for him to touch them. The disciples turned them away, but when Jesus saw this he was indignant and said to them, 'Let the little children come to me; do not stop them; for it is to such as these that the kingdom of God belongs. I tell you solemnly, anyone who does not welcome the kingdom of God like a little child will never enter it.' Then he put his arms round them, laid his hands on them and gave them his blessing.

This is the Gospel of the Lord.

READING 3

Our personal loss is such that we may find it difficult to see this child in the care of our Saviour. But God does not want to lose anyone, but to raise all to new life.

Gospel Acclamation   *Jn 6:39*

Alleluia, alleluia!
The will of my Father, says the Lord,
is that I should lose nothing
of all that he has given to me,
and that I should raise it up on the last day.
Alleluia!

A reading from the holy Gospel according to John   *6:37-40 Page 86*

It is my Father's will that I should lose nothing of all that he has given to me.

READING 4

The day of this child's first Holy Communion was one of great joy for us all. The fullness of that joy is in realising that it was the beginning of the eternal life he or she now enjoys.

Gospel Acclamation   *Jn 6:39*

Alleluia, alleluia!
The will of my Father, says the Lord,
is that I should lose nothing
of all that he has given to me,
and that I should raise it up on the last day.
Alleluia!

A reading from the holy Gospel according to John   *6:51-58 (Page 87)*

Anyone who eats this bread has eternal life, and I shall raise him up on the last day.

READING 5

Like the bystanders in this story we also ask if this death could not have been prevented. Jesus' answer is to ask us for more faith. Then we may be able to glimpse the glory given to this child now.

Gospel Acclamation   *2 Co 1:3-4*

Alleluia, alleluia!
Blessed be God, a gentle Father
and the God of all consolation,
who comforts us in all our sorrows.
Alleluia!

A reading from the holy Gospel according to John   *11:32-45*
                                                         Pages 89-90

If you believe, you will see the glory of God.

READING 6

The death of Jesus came when all had been done according to the Father's will. The death of each of us, early or late, comes when we are ripe for God's harvest. Yet God recognises how we suffer pain today with the parents of this child. Jesus was himself concerned for his mother in her grief.

Gospel Acclamation   *2 Cor 1:3-4*

Alleluia, alleluia!
Blessed be God, a gentle Father
and the God of all consolation,
who comforts us in all our sorrows.
Alleluia!

A reading from the holy Gospel according to John   *19:25-30*

This is your mother.

Near the cross of Jesus stood his mother and his mother's sister, Mary the wife of Clopas, and Mary of Magdala. Seeing his mother and the disciple he loved standing near her, Jesus said to his mother, 'Woman, this is your son'. Then to the disciple he said, 'This is your mother'. And from that moment the disciple made a place for her in his home. After this, Jesus knew that everything had now been completed, and to fulfil the scripture perfectly he said:
    'I am thirsty.'
A jar full of vinegar stood there, so putting a sponge soaked in vinegar on a hyssop stick they held it up to his mouth. After Jesus had taken the vinegar he said, 'It is accomplished'; and bowing his head he gave up his spirit.
    This is the Gospel of the Lord.

II Burial of Non-Baptised Children

Old Testament

READING I

God's all-embracing love will gather us all together in his kingdom, and there will be an end to all sorrow and grief.

A reading from the prophet Isaiah   25:6-8

The Lord will destroy Death for ever.

> On this mountain,
> the Lord of hosts will prepare for all peoples
> a banquet of rich food.
> On this mountain he will remove
> the mourning veil covering all peoples,
> and the shroud enwrapping all nations,
> he will destroy Death for ever.
> The Lord will wipe away
> the tears from every cheek.
>   This is the word of the Lord.

READING 2

The God who gave life to this child still shows his love. With quiet trust we know that his salvation is given in new life.

A reading from the Book of Lamentations   3:22-26

It is good to wait in silence for the Lord to save.

> The favours of the Lord are not all past,
> his kindnesses are not exhausted;
> every morning they are renewed;
> great is his faithfulness.
> 'My portion is the Lord' says my soul
> 'and so I will hope in him.'

The Lord is good to those who trust him,
to the soul that searches for him.
It is good to wait in silence
for the Lord to save.
    This is the Gospel of the Lord.

Gospels & Gospel Acclamations

READING I

Jesus tells us that the kingdom of God is revealed to little children. He asks us to trust him in the midst of our grief. God's love will take care of us all.

Gospel Acclamation   *Rv 1:5-6*

Alleluia, alleluia!
Jesus Christ is the First-born from the dead;
to him be glory and power for ever and ever. Amen.
Alleluia!

A reading from the holy Gospel according to Matthew   *11:25-30*

You have hidden these things from the clever, revealed them to mere children.

Jesus exclaimed, 'I bless you, Father, Lord of heaven and of earth, for hiding these things from the learned and the clever and revealing them to mere children. Yes, Father, for that is what it pleased you to do. Everything has been entrusted to me by my Father; and no one knows the Son except the Father, just as no one knows the Father except the Son and those to whom the Son chooses to reveal him.
'Come to me, all you who labour and are overburdened, and I will give you rest. Shoulder my yoke and learn from me, for I am gentle and humble in heart, and you will find rest for your souls. Yes, my yoke is easy and my burden light.'
    This is the Gospel of the Lord.

READING 2

The tragedy of death is such that even Jesus could cry out to the Father in desolation. This Gospel passage reminds us of the comfort his mother received from the friends who gave support in her hour of grief and loss.

Gospel Acclamation   *2 Co 1:3-4*

> Alleluia, alleluia!
> Blessed be God, a gentle Father
> and the God of all consolation,
> who comforts us in all our sorrows.
> Alleluia!

A reading from the holy Gospel according to Mark   *15:33-46*

Jesus gave a loud cry and breathed his last.

When the sixth hour came there was darkness over the whole land until the ninth hour. And at the ninth hour Jesus cried out in a loud voice, 'Eloi, Eloi, lama sabachthani?' which means, 'My God, my God, why have you deserted me?' When some of those who stood by heard this, they said, 'Listen, he is calling on Elijah'. Someone ran and soaked a sponge in vinegar and, putting it on a reed, gave it him to drink saying, 'Wait and see if Elijah will come to take him down'. But Jesus gave a loud cry and breathed his last. And the veil of the Temple was torn in two from top to bottom. The centurion, who was standing in front of him, had seen how he had died, and he said, 'In truth this man was a son of God.'

There were some women watching from a distance. Among them were Mary of Magdala, Mary who was the mother of James the younger and Joset, and Salome. These used to follow him and look after him when he was in Galilee. And there were many other women there who had come up to Jerusalem with him.

It was now evening, and since it was Preparation Day (that is, the vigil of the sabbath), there came Joseph of Arimathaea, a prominent member of the Council, who himself lived in the hope of seeing the kingdom of God, and he boldly went to Pilate and asked for the body of Jesus. Pilate, astonished that he should have died so soon, summoned the centurion and enquired if he was already dead. Having been as-

sured of this by the centurion, he granted the corpse to Joseph who bought a shroud, took Jesus down from the cross, wrapped him in the shroud and laid him in a tomb which had been hewn out of rock. He then rolled a stone against the entrance to the tomb.
> This is the Gospel of the Lord.

READING 3

We who are mourning the loss of this child should make a special place in our lives for the parents who suffer such a grievous loss. Like Jesus we have to be completely obedient to the Father who knows when each life has reached its fulfilment.

Gospel Acclamation   *2 Co 1:3-4*

> Alleluia, alleluia!
> Blessed be God, a gentle Father
> and the God of all consolation,
> who comforts us in all our sorrows.
> Alleluia!

A reading from the holy Gospel according to John   *19:25-30*

This is your mother.

Near the cross of Jesus stood his mother and his mother's sister, Mary the wife of Clopas, and Mary of Magdala. Seeing his mother and the disciple he loved standing near her, Jesus said to his mother, 'Woman, this is your son.' Then to the disciple he said, 'This is your mother.' And from that moment the disciple made a place for her in his home. After this, Jesus knew that everything had now been completed, and to fulfil the scripture perfectly he said:
  'I am thirsty.'
  A jar full of vinegar stood there, so putting a sponge soaked in the vinegar on a hyssop stick they held it up to his mouth. After Jesus had taken the vinegar he said, 'It is accomplished'; and bowing his head he gave up his spirit.
> This is the Gospel of the Lord.

FUNERAL PSALMS

1

Ps 22 R7. v. 1

If the psalm is not sung the following introduction may be used:

Christ, the good shepherd, leads us through the valley of darkness. We pray with and for our departed friend as we say:

R7. The Lord is my shepherd;
    there is nothing I shall want.

1. The Lord is my shepherd;
    there is nothing I shall want.
    Fresh and green are the pastures
    where he gives me repose.
    Near restful waters he leads me,
    to revive my drooping spirit. R7.

2. He guides me along the right path;
    he is true to his name.
    If I should walk in the valley of darkness
    no evil would I fear.
    You are there with your crook and your staff;
    with these you give me comfort. R7.

3. You have prepared a banquet for me
    in the sight of my foes.
    My head you have anointed with oil;
    my cup is overflowing. R7.

4. Surely goodness and kindness shall follow me
    all the days of my life.
    In the Lord's own house shall I dwell
    for ever and ever. R7.

2

Ps 24:4-7. 17. 20 R̂. v. 1. Alt. R̂. v.3

If the psalm is not sung the following introduction may be used:

We pray for freedom and eternal rest for N., and we are confident of God's faithfulness as we say:

R̂. To you, O Lord, I lift up my soul.
or
R̂. Those who hope in you, O Lord,
   shall not be disappointed.

1. Lord, make me know your ways.
   Lord, teach me your paths.
   Make me walk in your truth, and teach me:
   for you are god my saviour. R̂.

2. Remember your mercy, Lord,
   and the love you have shown from of old.
   In your love remember me
   because of your goodness, O Lord. R̂.

3. Relieve the anguish of my heart
   and set me free from my distress.
   Preserve my life and rescue me.
   Do not disappointment me, you are my refuge. R̂.

3

Ps 26:1. 4. 7-9. 13-14 R̂. v. 1. Alt. R̂. v. 13

If the psalm is not sung the following introduction may be used:

We pray that our departed friend may be brought into the house of the Lord as for him/her we say:

R̂. The Lord is my light and my help.
or

R7. I am sure I shall see the Lord's goodness
    in the land of the living.

1. The Lord is my light and my help;
   whom shall I fear?
   The Lord is the stronghold of my life;
   before whom shall I shrink? R7.

2. There is one thing I ask of the Lord,
   for this I long,
   to live in the house of the Lord,
   all the days of my life,
   to savour the sweetness of the Lord,
   to behold his temple. R7.

3. O Lord, hear my voice when I call;
   have mercy and answer.
   It is your face, O Lord, that I seek;
   hide not your face. R7.

4. I am sure I shall see the Lord's goodness
   in the land of the living.
   Hope in him, hold firm and take heart.
   Hope in the Lord! R7.

4

Pss 41:2-3. 5; 42:3-5 R7. Ps 41:3

If the psalm is not sung the following introduction may be used:

This psalm of desire for the presence of God becomes our prayer for the departed as we say:

R7. My soul is thirsting for God,
    the God of my life.

1. Like the deer that yearns
   for running streams,
   so my soul is yearning
   for you, my God. R7.

2. My soul is thirsting for God,
   the God of my life;
   when can I enter and see
   the face of God? Ry.

3. These things will I remember
   as I pour out my soul:
   how I would lead the rejoicing crowd
   into the house of God,
   amid cries of gladness and thanksgiving,
   the throng wild with joy. Ry.

4. O send forth your light and your truth;
   let these be my guide.
   Let them bring me to your holy mountain,
   to the place where you dwell. Ry.

5. And I will come to the altar of God,
   the God of my joy.
   My redeemer, I will thank you on the harp,
   O God, my God. Ry.

6. Why are you cast down, my soul,
   why groan within me?
   Hope in God; I will praise him still,
   my saviour and my God. Ry.

5

Ps 62:2-6. 8-9 Ry. v. 2

If the psalm is not sung the following introduction may be used:

In death we are freed to love God without hindrance; our response expresses desire for that total union with God.

Ry. For you my soul is thirsting,
   O Lord, my God.

1. O God, you are my God, for you I long;
   for you my soul is thirsting.

My body pines for you
like a dry, weary land without water. R℞.

2. So I gaze on you in the sanctuary
   to see your strength and your glory.
   For your love is better than life,
   my lips will speak your praise. R℞.

3. So I will bless you all my life,
   in your name I will lift up my hands.
   My soul shall be filled as with a banquet,
   my mouth shall praise you with joy. R℞.

4. You have been my help;
   in the shadow of your wings I rejoice.
   My soul clings to you;
   your right hand holds me fast. R℞.

6

Ps 102:8. 10. 13-18 R℞. v. 8. Alt. R℞. Ps 36:39

If the psalm is not sung the following introduction may be used:

As we mourn for N. we can trust that he is at peace with a loving Father; we express our confidence as we say:

R℞. The Lord is compassion and love.
or
R℞. The salvation of the just
     comes from the Lord.

1. The Lord is compassion and love,
   slow to anger and rich in mercy.
   He does not treat us according to our sins
   nor repay us according to our faults. R℞.

2. As a father has compassion on his sons,
   the Lord has pity on those who fear him;

for he knows of what we are made,
he remembers that we are dust. R7.

3. As for man, his days are like grass;
   he flowers like the flower of the field;
   the wind blows and he is gone
   and his place never sees him again. R7.

4. But the love of the Lord is everlasting
   upon those who hold him in fear;
   his justice reaches out to children's children
   when they keep his covenant in truth. R7.

7

Pss 114:5-6; 115:10-11. 15-16 R7. Ps 114:9

If the psalm is not sung the following introduction may be used:

The psalm expresses simple trust in God at the moment of death; in that trust and with faith we say:

R7. I will walk in the presence of the Lord
     in the land of the living.
or
R7. Alleluia!

1. How gracious is the Lord, and just;
   our God has compassion.
   The Lord protects the simple hearts;
   I was helpless so he saved me. R7.

2. I trusted, even when I said:
   'I am sorely afflicted,'
   and when I said in my alarm:
   'No man can be trusted.' R7.

3. O precious in the eyes of the Lord
   is the death of his faithful.

Your servant, Lord, your servant am I;
you have loosened my bonds. R℣.

8

Ps 121 R℣. v. 1. Alt. R℣. cf. v. 1

If the psalm is not sung the following introduction may be used:

Death is another stage on the pilgrim journey to the house of the Lord; we re-
joice with N. coming into the presence of God as we say:

R℣. I rejoiced when I heard them say;
   'Let us go to God's house.'
or
R℣. Let us go to God's house, rejoicing.

1. I rejoiced when I heard them say:
   'Let us go to God's house.'
   And now our feet are standing
   within your gates, O Jerusalem. R℣.

2. Jerusalem is built as a city
   strongly compact.
   It is there that the tribes go up,
   and tribes of the Lord. R℣.

3. For Israel's law it is,
   there to praise the Lord's name.
   There were set the thrones of judgment
   of the house of David. R℣.

4. For the peace of Jerusalem pray:
   'Peace be to your homes!
   May peace reign in your walls,
   in your palaces, peace!' R℣.

5. For love of my brethren and friends
   I say: 'Peace upon you!'

For love of the house of the Lord
I will ask for your good. R℣

9

Ps 129 R℣. v. 1. Alt. R℣. cf. v. 5

If the psalm is not sung the following introduction may be used:

We become the voice of our departed friend as, with faith in God's immense mercy, we say:

R℣. Out of the depths, I cry to you, O Lord.
or
R℣. I wait for the Lord,
      I count on his word.

1. Out of the depths I cry to you, O Lord,
   Lord, hear my voice!
   O let your ears be attentive
   to the voice of my pleading. R℣.

2. If you, O Lord, should mark our guilt,
   Lord, who would survive?
   But with you is found forgiveness;
   for this we revere you. R℣.

3. My soul is waiting for the Lord,
   I count on his word.
   My soul is longing for the Lord
   more than watchman for daybreak.R℣.

4. Because with the Lord there is mercy
   and fullness of redemption,
   Israel indeed he will redeem
   from all its iniquity. R℣.

10

Ps 142: 1-2. 5-8. 10 R℟. v. 1

If the psalm is not sung the following introduction may be used:

This psalm prays for God's mercy and love in his judgements; with trust we say:

R℟. Lord, listen to my prayer.

1. Lord, listen to my prayer:
   turn your ear to my appeal.
   You are faithful, you are just; give answer.
   Do not call your servant to judgment
   for no one is just in your sight. R℟.

2. I remember the days that are past:
   I ponder all your works.
   I muse on what your hand has wrought
   and to you I stretch out my hands.
   Like a parched land my soul thirsts for you. R℟.

3. Lord, make haste and give me answer;
   for my spirit fails within me.
   In the morning let me know your love
   for I put my trust in you. R℟.

4. Teach me to do your will,
   for you, O Lord, are my God.
   Let your good spirit guide me
   in ways that are level and smooth. R℟.

11

Ps 24:6-7.17-18. 20-21 R℟. v. 1. Alt. R℟. v. 3

If the psalm is not sung the following introduction may be used:

(Children)
We put the innocence and sinlessness of this child before God as a plea
for protection as we say:

R̞. To you, O Lord, I lift up my soul.
or
R̞. Those who hope in you, O Lord,
      shall not be disappointed.

1. Remember your mercy, Lord,
      and the love you have shown from of old.
   In your love remember me,
      because of your goodness, O Lord. R̞.

2. Relieve the anguish of my heart
      and set me free from my distress.
   See my affliction and my toil
      and take all my sins away. R̞.

3. Preserve my life and rescue me.
      Do not disappoint me, you are my refuge.
   May innocence and uprightness protect me:
      for my hope is in you, O Lord. R̞.

12

Ps 148:1-2. 11-14 R̞. v. 13

If the psalm is not sung the following introduction may be used:

The child we mourn joins with the angels and saints in the eternal praise
of God; let us join our voices to that song as we say:

R̞. Praise the name of the Lord.
or
R̞. Alleluia!

1. Praise the Lord from the heavens,
      praise him in the heights.

Praise him, all his angels,
praise him, all his host. R7.

2. All earth's kings and peoples,
earth's princes and rulers;
young men and maidens,
old men together with children. R7.

3. Let them praise the name of the Lord
for he alone is exalted.
The splendour of his name
reaches beyond heaven and earth. R7.

4. He exalts the strength of his people.
He is the praise of all his saints,
of the sons of Israel,
of the people to whom he comes close. R7.

Other Scriptural Readings

Psalm 90

He who dwells in the shelter of the Most High
and abides in the shade of the Almighty
says to the Lord: 'My refuge,
my stronghold, my God in whom I trust!'

It is he who will free you from the snare
of the fowler who seeks to destroy you;
he will conceal you with his pinions
and under his wings you will find refuge.

You will not fear the terror of the night
nor the arrow that flies by day,
nor the plague that prowls in the darkness
nor the scourge that lays waste at noon.

A thousand may fall at your side,
ten thousand fall at your right;
you, it will never approach;
his faithfulness is buckler and shield.

Your eyes have only to look
to see how the wicked are repaid,
you who have said: 'Lord, my refuge!'
and have made the Most High your dwelling.

Upon you no evil shall fall,
no plague approach where you dwell.
For you has he commanded his angels,
to keep you in all your ways.

They shall bear you upon their hands
lest you strike you foot against a stone.
On the lion and the viper you will tread
and trample the young lion and the dragon.

His love he set on me, so I will rescue him;
protect him for he knows my name.
When he calls I shall answer: 'I am with you.'
I will save him in distress and give him glory.

With length of life I will content him;
I shall let him see my saving power.

A reading from the first letter of John   *4:16*

God's love for us.

We ourselves have known and put our faith in
God's love towards ourselves.
God is love
and anyone who lives in love lives in God,
and God lives in him.
      This is the Gospel of the Lord.

A reading from the Book of Revelation   *21:1-7 Page 64*

*God our Father is the God of newness and life; it is his desire that we should
come to share his life with him.*

A reading from the holy Gospel according to Luke   *22:39-46*

*Jesus is alive to our pain and sorrow, because faithfulness to his Father's will
cost him life itself.*

Jesus left to make his way as usual to the Mount of Olives, with the
disciples following. When they reached the place he said to them,
'Pray not to be put to the test.'
Then he withdrew from them, about a stone's throw away, and knelt
down and prayed. 'Father,' he said, 'if you are willing, take this cup
away from me. Nevertheless, let your will be done, not mine.' Then
an angel appeared to him, coming from heaven to give him strength.

In his anguish he prayed even more earnestly, and his sweat fell to the ground like great drops of blood.

When he rose from prayer he went to the disciples and found them sleeping for sheer grief. 'Why are you asleep?' he said to them. 'Get up and pray not to be put to the test.'

This is the Gospel of the Lord.

A reading from the holy Gospel according to Luke   23:44-49

Jesus' death is witnessed by his friends.

It was now about the sixth hour and, with the sun eclipsed, a darkness came over the whole land until the ninth hour. The veil of the Temple was torn right down the middle; and when Jesus had cried out in a loud voice, he said, 'Father, into your hands I commit my spirit'. With these words he breathed his last.

When the centurion saw what had taken place, he gave praise to God and said, 'This was a great and good man'. And when all the people who had gathered for the spectacle saw what had happened, they went home beating their breasts.

All his friends stood at a distance; so also did the women who had accompanied him from Galilee, and they saw all this happen.

This is the Gospel of the Lord.

A reading from the holy Gospel according to Luke   24:1-8

Jesus is alive; he gives us eternal life with the Father.

On the first day of the week, at the first sign of dawn, the women went to the tomb with the spices they had prepared. They found that the stone had been rolled away from the tomb, but on entering discovered that the body of the Lord Jesus was not there. As they stood there not knowing what to think, two men in brilliant clothes suddenly appeared at their side. Terrified, the women lowered their eyes. But the two men said to them, 'Why look among the dead for someone who is alive? He is not here; he has risen. Remember what he told you when he was still in Galilee: that the Son of Man had to be handed over into the power of sinful men and be crucified, and rise again on the third day.' And they remembered his words.

This is the Gospel of the Lord.

A reading from the holy Gospel according to John

11:3-7.17. 20-27.33-35.41b-44

The sisters sent this message to Jesus, 'Lord, the man you love is ill'. On receiving the message, Jesus said, 'This sickness will end not in death but in God's glory, and through it the Son of God will be glorified'.
Jesus loved Martha and her sister and Lazarus, yet when he heard that Lazarus was ill he stayed where he was for two more days before saying to the disciples, 'Let us go to Judaea'.
On arriving, Jesus found that Lazarus had been in the tomb for four days already. When Martha heard that Jesus had come she went to meet him. Mary remained sitting in the house. Martha said to Jesus, 'If you had been here, my brother would not have died, but I know that, even now, whatever you ask of God, he will grant you.' 'Your brother' said Jesus to her 'will rise again.' Martha said, 'I know he will rise again at the resurrection on the last day.' Jesus said:

'I am the resurrection and the life.
If anyone believes in me, even though he dies he will live,
and whoever lives and believes in me
will never die.
Do you believe this?'

'Yes, Lord,' she said 'I believe that you are the Christ, the Son of God, the one who was to come into this world.'
At the sight of her tears, and those of the Jews who followed her, Jesus said in great distress, with a sigh that came straight from the heart, 'Where have you put him?' They said, 'Lord, come and see.' Jesus wept; and the Jews said, 'See how much he loved him!' Then Jesus lifted up his eyes and said:

'Father, I thank you for hearing my prayer.
I knew indeed that you always hear me,
but I speak
for the sake of all these who stand round me,
so that they may believe it was you who sent me.'

When he had said this, he cried in a loud voice, 'Lazarus, here! Come out!' The dead man came out, his feet and hands bound with bands of stuff and a cloth round his face. Jesus said to them, 'Unbind him, let him go free'.
This is the Gospel of the Lord.

Index of Readings and Psalms